1

BUSINESS DiVA

This book is a compilation of stories from numerous people who have each contributed a chapter and is designed to provide inspiration to our readers.

It is sold with the understanding that the publisher and the individual authors are not engaged in the rendering of psychological, legal, accounting or other professional advice. The content and views in each chapter are the sole expression and opinion of its author and not necessarily the views of Fig Factor Media, LLC.

For more information, contact:

Fig Factor Media, LLC | www.figfactormedia.com
Business Divas Worldwide | www.businessdivaseries.com

Cover Design by DG Marco Alvarez
Layout by LDG Juan Manuel Serna Rosales

Printed in the United States of America

ISBN: 978-1-959989-09-7
Library of Congress Control Number: XX

FIG
FACTOR
MEDIA

This book is dedicated to all women who are seeking to start a business and for those who have already started one. To the young girl who has been told she is only meant to be a stay-at-home mom, to the immigrant child who has been overlooked, to any women who have been told they are not enough. I want this book to inspire you to find your own purpose and abundance through your own entrepreneurship path. If this is not your path, open your heart and mind to be enlightened.

TABLE OF CONTENTS

Acknowledgements

I want to acknowledge all twenty-two women who were open and vulnerable to share their journey in becoming business owners and be part of this future worldwide book series. Nothing in life is easy. Being a business owner comes with many challenges, many points that make one feel exhausted and hopeless, but behind any challenge are the fruits to success.

I want to thank my parents, Agustin Razo and Maria T. Razo, who have allowed me and trusted me to run our family business. I thank my father for mentoring me not only in life but in business. I am able to lead in a men-dominated industry thanks to all his lessons, which, if I am being honest, didn't always make sense growing up.

I want to thank my husband, Thomas Vazquez, for being by my side in everything and accompanying me in the long stretch of publishing this amazing book. I want to thank my son, Angelo Vazquez, for making me even more of a superwoman by making me a mother. Angelo is the light of my life. I want him to know that he is capable of anything he can imagine.

Lastly, thanks to my publisher, Fig Factor Media, and their team for their incredible work in putting this revolutionary book, *Business Diva,* together.

INTRODUCTION
By Martha Razo

A Business Diva is resilient, persistent, courageous, witty, kind, and charming all at once.

A Business Diva is passionate about her work, she has found her purpose and works diligently and with discipline. As the Latin word implies, *DIVA* means she is a goddess. She shows greatness and leadership in her respective business industry, and most importantly, her vision and work impacts others' lives for the greater good. She is humble and shares with others her success. Some may call a Business Diva a superwoman, since she quickly adapts and solves any problems from home and her business. A Business Diva shines light to what we are all capable of.

I am proud to bring together twenty-two amazing women to share their stories in this incredible book. These businesswomen represent different industries, ages, cultures, and segments of their business journeys. These Business Divas come from different parts of the world and they are in different stages of their businesses. Some are developing their startups, some have built empires, others are selling their companies. The mission is to inspire all women and those who read their stories to follow their own purpose and encourage them to achieve success through entrepreneurship. The authors open themselves and share the reality of what they went through to be where they are today. My hope as you read these narratives is that you learn from their successes and failures and know that you are not alone. The struggles you have and are enduring are perhaps some that they also have gone through.

According to the US Department of Labor Women's Bureau Data and Statistics[1], in 2021 there was around a 17 percent gap between men and women's annual pay. Even in leadership roles, only 24 percent of CEOs in the US were women and they earned 74.5 percent of what male CEOs earned.[2] This data should motivate us all to turn the tables and change these numbers. Women are powerhouses, and it's up to us to be part of this shift. The best way to combat inequality in pay for women is to start your own business. The answer to creating a worldwide movement of women living their purpose and thriving on their terms is through entrepreneurship.

Business Diva is here to share the stories of women taking their futures and lives into their own hands. It's for all women who are interested in business and wonder: *What if there is more out there for me?* It's for those that have been told they can't or have had doors closed on them. It's for those who are tired of their nine-to-five jobs and want to build a legacy of their own and for those that are looking for motivation. This book will make you cry, laugh, and, more importantly, it will inspire you and plant the seed for you to start your own empire and grow your dreams.

[1] "Gender Earnings Ratios by Weekly and Annual Earnings." United States Department of Labor. Accessed November 28, 2022. https://www.dol.gov/agencies/wb/data/earnings/gender-ratio-weekly-annual.
[2] BLS 2010. "Highlights of Women's Earnings in 2009," Washington, DC. Accessed November 28, 2022. http://www.bls.gov/cps/cpswom2009.pdf

PREFACE
By Marie Antonette G. Waite

Branding Strategist/Radio Producer/TV Director

As I reflect on my career, I can't help but think about the pivotal moments that led me to where I am today. The stories in this book share many similar moments, emotions, challenges, and victories that I, too, experienced as an entrepreneur and business owner. I understand firsthand the impact that our work and services provide to others.

In my line of work—as a brand strategist and expert—I provide ideas, opportunities, connections, and powerful marketing programs that help build business and personal branding for business professionals, entrepreneurs, and business owners. I love the opportunity of creating a unique positioning within the industry and using the Pull Marketing method to attract their target market and build their lifetime referrals.

My expertise comes from a decades-long career in various industries such as real estate investment and development, health care, marketing, and the fashion industry. Persistence and dedication are some of my inner qualities on how I envision and execute the service to my clients and complete projects. Having the love, fun, and passion in everything I do is a must. I stand firm with my business and personal principles in life in regards to respect, trust, and quality of work. I aim for the best and never hesitate in achieving it. Having the strength to fulfill my callings in serving others gives me the reward that I need to exist in this world. My love for GOD and my relationship with him gives me the power of wisdom and creativity.

In my life, I have been inspired by my grandfather, who was the founder of karate in the Philippines; my uncle and my dad, who made hundreds of karate movies in the Philippines; and my mother, who was the first female karate black belter and the first female who performed a karate exhibition on television. I come from a line of incredible people, and I take my legacy seriously. My family brings me immense joy, and I have endless love for my daughter, who is finishing her sixth year in college while working two jobs and also raising her child. I also love my son, who has been dedicated and has accomplished amazing things like being the number one wide receiver in high school and now receiving a scholarship from Walsh University as one of their best football players. These moments make me so proud and inspire me to continue reaching for success as a Filipino American woman. I am living my ancestors' wildest dreams!

To me, the meaning of *Business Divas* means being resilient, committed, and believing in yourself with a purpose. Believing your vision of why you exist and how you can bless others to be strong and powerful. Embrace your unique perspective in life on how it can create a beautiful vision for you in serving others. Being a Business Diva means always finding something inspirational for others and for yourself. It brings out the best in you and will bring forth great discoveries of your hidden talents. Enjoy God's masterful work within you by learning all the abilities that you have been gifted and how you can bless others with your gifts.

These stories told in this book need to be shared. To the contributing authors, don't miss the opportunity of inspiring someone with your story. I am proud of your vulnerability and desire to make an impact with your story. Maybe it will never be perfect in your eyes, or you feel the need to overanalyze it. But remember, you made it happen, and you will be blessed by your work in inspiring other people. Embrace your qualities and deeply understand your talents to then focus on serving people selflessly. Being a woman is a big factor of who you are and how you can envision yourself as someone that can make a difference to others.

To our readers, I hope you learn and take away wonderful and powerful lessons of courage, overcoming, and following your dreams from this book. Be bold, courageous, and be fearless. You were made perfectly and made for a purpose! Love yourself as well as loving others. Be grateful to GOD as he made you, and he has great plans for you to be the best that you can be. Always smile and brand yourself with great vision! The reward for yourself is to serve other people and lead them to a successful journey with your talent and creativity. God will always be there to assist you with all of his almighty power!

Congratulations to you for being a part of this amazing contribution!

Marie Antonette G. Waite

Founder and CEO of Finest Women in Real Estate, LLC, Fire-Up Connect, and Real Men of Real Estate

Founder and Board Member, Inland Valley Business and Community Foundation, Inc.

Advisory Board Member for WCTE, Inc.

Program Advisor for UCR Riverside Transformational Leadership

Director of Global Society For Female Entrepreneurs - Central San Diego

A WOMAN LEADING IN A MAN'S INDUSTRY

MARTHA RAZO

"You are the only one that can set your own limits, so let's make your future limitless!"

BEHIND A CLOSED DOOR, YOU WILL FIND THE DOOR TO YOUR SUCCESS.

My first experience with business started when I was a sophomore in high school, in a very uncommon arena, a nonprofit.

I was born in Michoacan, Mexico. I am the oldest of four siblings, three brothers and one sister. I used to say that I was the only one with the "curse" of being undocumented.

Later in life, I realized that my legal status made me a fighter and persistent in making my dreams a reality.

My legal status presented many barriers along the way. My own teachers and peers constantly told me to stop working so hard that I could not go to college. However, I was not the person to take no for an answer. This is important for the reader to note: no one knows everything other than God, so always cross-check any "facts." Do not take no for an answer; find your own door. Many doors will close, but behind a closed door, you will find the door to your success.

I looked for my own door to success to get a higher education, regardless of legal status. I visited many not-for-profits that advocated for immigrant rights, searched online, and even interviewed community leaders regarding immigration rights. Vola, I discovered that even as an immigrant, I could attend college, and although I could not apply for FAFSA, there are several scholarships for undocumented students.

I took a step further and started by taking the first steps into learning about business. I had a mission to educate and help other undocumented students like myself achieve their dream of higher education.

At only fifteen years of age, I pitched my idea to start a scholarship for undocumented students to Universidad Popular, a nonprofit whose mission is "Education with, by and for the people." They loved the idea! But like many nonprofits, they were limited on resources and gave me the baton to lead the project.

Whenever you start a business, the first step is to have a clear mission that others believe in. I gathered my team members to help me with this life-changing project. I led four other high school students who believed in the mission. Students for Students Scholarship was born! Now with my team, I had to develop leadership skills and allow each person to do what they are good at to make the *Students for Students Scholarship* a reality.

We planned and organized several fundraising events, from raffles and asking for donations to annual events. We organized a large Winter Craft Fair. Our first event brought in over four hundred people. It was a success, and high school students organized this. The power was the team and sharing a common goal to raise money for scholarships to support undocumented students' dreams of attending college. We recruited more volunteers that even included my younger brother, Rafael.

We went canvassing door to door in the Little Village community to educate families that undocumented students could attend college; we also informed them about the *Students for Students Scholarship*. We were probably given about $20 in donations in total, but what was incredible was that we brought hope and a wealth of information to the immigrant families we visited. Overall, we raised over $7,000 in two years. We were able to award over eight scholarships to undocumented students within two years.

I had to stop because the reality came when I had to apply for college. However, my project had to pause. I had forgotten about myself. In my selfless act of helping others, I forgot that I would be going to college.

FROM CLEANING SAWDUST TO BUILDING A NATIONAL COMPANY

I was enrolled at the Illinois Institute of Technology, majoring in applied mathematics. It was great to be admitted to college, but I had a yearly tuition of $12,000. How was I going to pay for that? At that time, I was no longer living with my parents, and at eighteen, I chose to live with my boyfriend.

I felt my hands were chained and my feet were planted under cement. My world was caught in a small box where the light did not shine. The high pitch of the counselor rattled my ears when she told me, "Martha, you do not qualify for financial aid from the government." My chest was drying up, trying to hold in the tears of desperation. Was the path to success closing now on me? Are my straight As now scraps of hope?

Suddenly, I realized that I was not living the daily struggles of my ancestors, walking on a rocky surface with twelve children or suffering cold, rainy days. My obstacle was surely minor. I did not want to endure like the past generations; education was my passion and the path to triumph in life. I was not going to take NO for an answer and decided to pursue college anyway. With time, I realized that there is one treasure everyone has access to: knowledge.

I worked at Chipotle for a year. My father had his own business, Guero's Pallets, a pallet-recycling plant. When I was young, I used to climb the stacks of pallets and hide from my father from making me work. I wanted to work for him, but I had not been on good terms since I left home. I decided to talk to my father and ask him for a job! I was terrified to approach him, since I knew he was very disappointed and upset that I had left home. Surprisingly, my father allowed me to work on his pallet plan. He had forgiven me and gave me the opportunity to work.

When I started, I was assigned to clean the warehouse. I cleaned the sawdust and picked up the boards and stringers that fell off the bundles. I was later trained to use the baker machine to thin out the stringers to deck boards. I learned to operate the saw machine used for cutting boards and stringers (the individual pieces to build the pallets). I also learned how to manage the forklift to load and unload trucks. I worked for about a year inside the warehouse with all the guys. I was good; I was cutting over seven bundles of boards daily, more than some of the guys would cut.

However, I soon realized I could not work inside the warehouse for my entire life. I was pursuing a math degree; there had to be something I could do to help Guero's Pallets expand. I asked my father if I could learn office work and help him with business. When I entered the office, I quickly wanted to turn back; my father had a shoebox method for storing invoices and receipts.

I had a strong background in numbers and mathematics, but I had no idea how to organize and manage business accounts. I was given access to bank accounts and all the books. It was real; at only eighteen years old, I had to run the office of an entire pallet company. I learned to use QuickBooks, accounting software, and became QuickBooks Pro Certified.

Later, in 2015, I began to manage accounts and help dispatch drivers and coordinate their routes to optimize the number of loads delivered daily. Having a math degree, I was always thrilled to analyze reports and set financial goals for the company.

In 2016, I began formulating and implementing strategic planning to increase sales and expand the business. I was involved in purchasing an almost three-acre warehousing space that allowed for Guero's Pallets expansion. I became vice president, and one of my roles as VP was to develop business and financial plans and create forecasting models using statistics tools to ensure sales and profit goals were met.

It was not easy at the beginning; the pallet industry is male-dominated. Many men initially intended to either flirt with me or looked down at me, since I was much younger than them and a woman. Today I am respected and even admired by many of the men who lacked respect for me. Many of my competitors have asked me, "Martha, what is the secret to success?!" Keep reading, and I will reveal some of my secrets.

In 2020, when many businesses were struggling, our sales and profits kept growing. In 2021, using data-driven decisions, our company doubled in sales to $10.1 million, and our earnings increased from 5 percent to 35 percent. Even as I am writing this story, our company continues to grow. We have produced and expanded by buying an empty 1.45-acre land which we strategically are leasing. We have expanded nationwide, producing pallet solutions for over twenty starters over the United States. I have created a National Pallet Leaders group, for which I have an extensive agenda. I cannot reveal much, but many exciting projects are coming to Guero's Pallets and our expansion. This year we are projected to further increase our sales.

HELPING BUSINESS OWNERS CREATE THEIR OWN EMPIRE

My favorite industry is pallets! Pallets have given me the opportunities I have today. They have put food on my family's table. Moreover, pallets move the world; anything you physically hold has been shipped on a pallet. Even more impressive, pallets are 100 percent recycled and are a sustainable shipping and logistics option. The world rotates on pallets! I have been working for Guero's Pallets since 2014. Guero's Pallets is my family's company that buys, sells, recycles, and manufactures wood pallets. I am very grateful for the opportunity my father gave me in mentoring me and allowing me to become the strong business woman I am today.

After the pandemic, many businesses lost their companies. What saddened me was to see small, family-owned business owners close their doors. That could have easily been our pallet company.

Of course, I began to question why this was happening to others, not us. It broke my heart to see and hear in the news that the children of the parents and employees were in despair that their work was put to an end. Owning a business is a serious matter; you have so many people depending on you as a leader and owner of a company. Your family is directly affected, and the chain continues with your employees. Your employees' families will also be indirectly affected by your business closing or succeeding.

With a little push from a friend, I realized I had a gift I had been developing since I was fifteen, raising money for undocumented students to grow Guero's Pallets into a multimillion-dollar company. I am a business expert! I could save many small business owners and allow them to stay open and grow their companies.

In 2022, my mission began to use all my talents from mathematics, being a statistician, business expert, financial coach, and an engineer, to start my own consulting firm, SOLiX Business Services, with the mission to multiply business using data-driven strategies, the same I used to grow Guero's Pallets into a multimillion-dollar company. If you are a business owner looking for a coach, a second opinion, and growing your business, I will be a great source to start with.

HOW MARTHA BUILT A MULTIMILLION-DOLLAR COMPANY

Now, as I promised, what is the secret to business success? If you have a business idea in mind, make sure it is what you love. Would you continue to follow this path if you did not get paid for it? Secondly, facts show that small businesses have a short life. Less than 30 percent of small businesses make it over the ten-year mark. What does this mean, that being passionate about your business is not enough to be successful? One of the main reasons many business owners do not make the three-year mark, the five-year mark, or even the ten-year mark is poor cash management.

Many of us grow up okay with poor math skills and even hating numbers. But I must tell you that one of the secrets to my success has been my strength in understanding numbers, making decisions using data, forecasting, and creating strategies based on the data.

So, I will be straightforward: the fundamentals of business are numbers. You have to know your business numbers to be in business. This starts with understanding business reports. This is very important, so I started *The Power of Numbers* course, which I deliver twice a year. The objective is to teach business owners the key numbers for their business success and how to interpret and use them to grow their business. They are then connected to capital opportunities, such as private investors and banks, to expand their empires further.

Lastly, the last secret to success is to keep dreaming big, and set your goals high because you will reach higher horizons than you have thought if you set your goals too low.

I will summarize that business success comes from sharing that passion with a team that believes in your mission, knowing business numbers to create strategy using the data, and setting high business goals! Let's make your future limitless!

My Business Diva Final Word:

LiMITLESS

ERICA PRISCILLA SANDOVAL, LCSW

"You just have to begin."

SUNFLOWER

I ran payroll tonight, and it was hard. I always get anxious before I run payroll. I pay consultants at the end of each month, and it's painful to see the money that was earned leave my bank account. Money comes in, and it goes out. I noticed an uneasy feeling in my body. It starts with my shoulders, then my neck, and pretty soon, it goes down my back.

I went for a massage tonight. I also decided to decompress and really focus on my manifestations for my business. I told myself, be proud; the fact that you have a payroll to run means you are in business, Queen. But it always feels like a gasp for air after holding my breath.

I knew I wanted to be a CEO as soon as I learned what CEO meant—chief executive officer. The title was so enticing. It meant I was in charge, the boss, and had people reporting to me. Little did I know it would take me for a rollercoaster ride. The ups and downs and unspoken struggles of people in that position were hardly shared or taught at NYU Silver School of Social Work.

Growing up as an immigrant from Ecuador in Queens, NY, was tough. The neighborhood was predominantly Italian and Greek, and seldom did you see Ecuadorian business owners. We were usually working in factories, cleaning homes, delivering packages, or providing childcare for other people with more money and power. It seemed as if we were powerless, but that is not the case. I learned a lot during that time. Seeing my grandmother and mother maneuver through life with a business mind was priceless.

I watched *my abuelita* and mother negotiate their rates and hustle. These women used their *personalismo* and became matriarchs of our family. Guess what I do now? Negotiate my rates and hustle. It's hard at the start. I barely understood how to submit a proposal, much less marketing and social media. I just know my craft: mental health, wellness with an equity agenda. I am an advocate, healer, mental health provider, trainer, author, public speaker, and entrepreneur. I am not a CFO or a marketing expert, and I definitely do not want to sit in front of the computer, learning slews of online business systems. I just want to do what I love—help others heal.

But being an entrepreneur isn't just about doing the things you're good at. When you start your journey into entrepreneurship, you'll feel distressed, fearful, and anxious. You'll doubt yourself and say, "I can't do this!" Some days, you'll even want to give up and close down shop.

Those are the days when all that you can do is stop, step away, and get some rest. You might need it more than you think. It took me a long time to learn how to rest. I started to lose people because I couldn't focus on anything outside of my businesses. Without self-care, you won't be able to sustain the long journey that is your business. With rest, you will find clarity.

With clarity, you will be able to make better decisions. But how do we find clarity? Well, you begin by being honest with yourself. Ask yourself the really hard questions, and don't mask the problem. Why am I doing this? What is my end game? What is my purpose? Your purpose is your why. Holding onto the reason you do what you do will gain you clarity.

But clarity doesn't necessarily translate to a business plan, and that's nothing to be ashamed of. I eventually realized that writing a business plan simply isn't in my skill set. Just because you are in business, it doesn't mean you have the skill to put together the plan. You may have the vision but can't put it on paper. THAT IS OKAY! Don't be afraid to ask for help. Don't be afraid to invest in yourself, in YOUR business. Your business plan does not have to be the first thing you do. That is a myth. It sometimes takes time to really see your vision, and I realized I had to be in it for some time to really understand the impact I wanted to make and the direction I wanted to take.

"What is holding me back from committing to asking for help from experts in what I do not know how to do?" Perhaps you feel if you ask for help, you'll look like you don't know what you're doing. Perhaps it's your feelings of inadequacy. When we ask for help, we're saying, "I don't know if I can do this alone." That is exactly true!

We don't have to go to it alone, Queens! But we do have to be strategic. Bring in a team that has the skill sets you lack, and have them do the work you struggle with or just don't have enough time in the day to do. This will help you get organized, work on your craft, and deliver the services or products you provide.

Surround yourself with amazing humans who support your work. Sometimes it may look like your close family and friends, and sometimes it won't. It may be the person you met who shares the same struggles. You will have to look for the sunflowers in your life. They will be the people who are loyal, optimistic, honest, happy to help, and able to share their admiration of you. They will be your guides and light. They will turn with you as you shine, and you will radiate and mirror them because you will bloom. Have you ever seen a sunflower alone? Never.

HORSE

Since I launched my business, the money I've earned has stayed in the business and paid itself to continue to grow. I was working part time and making $80–100k, and that was sustaining me and my family. The money my business was making stayed in the business.

So, what does "stayed in the business" mean? It means you have to invest in your baby. This is your vision, and you will need to set goals and have people to support you. You will need someone to help you organize your thoughts, and that person is not your best friend. Hire a business coach, someone who is able to put your thoughts on paper. This will help you build a map. Though your best friends can be your listening ear, definitely work with a coach or join an entrepreneur group and seek mentors. I have joined affinity groups and even became a socia for Latina Empire in NYC. They are aligned with who I am and what I believe in. You first must grow personally to grow professionally. All the work you do will be worth it.

I have worked seven days a week and over twelve-hour days at times, but it does not feel like work, because it is mine, and I love it! I see myself as a horse that is free to do what she loves. I am strong, powerful, and have incredible stamina. Since I launched my first business, I have learned it takes stamina and strength. It can be depleting, and there is no guarantee. This is why I work so hard—because I know that, and the fear of failing is real. But we do fail at times. I know I have.

What is your mission, and what is the value you bring? My mission is to help as many people as possible be the best version of themselves. I am a true believer that healing is personal, and there are many ways of doing so. Reading, talking, writing, sharing in community, creating, having your *limpias,* your cards read, even talking to your spiritual guides. I'm all in for all of it with my clients and community.

BIRCH TREE

This is not a fairy tale. It is the real deal. Money changes everything. While investing in a social media coordinator, applying for grants, and having a full caseload, I began to see what I was struggling with.

I have always been a child facing the sun. I would shine and light up the room from a very early age. It was a natural talent for me. I never tried, I just existed in spaces and did not fear the unknown. I remember being six years old, walking into a classroom with limited English, and making friends that same day. While other kids were crying and silently in despair, my goal was to connect and make friends—and I did. My first best friend, Jennifer Giron, can testify to this. We're still connected.

I recall wanting to make people feel good, and I genuinely wanted to see them happy. Once friends, my loyalty was the key to successful relationships. For the most part, I was a pretty happy little being. I had a smile and laugh that were contagious, and I loved to play. I really loved to play. There was this joy in me that people strive for and pay lots of money to obtain as adults. It's the pure essence of happiness.

Life gets in the way and can dim your light at times, and though I experienced multiple traumas, I always protected that light. That light helped me build and nurtured me to become a leader and healer. I see myself as a birch tree, known as a tree of beginnings. I began over and over again throughout my life, and have given birth to many ideas and dreams.

I have had multiple career shifts, from the music industry, to hospitality, to health care, to nonprofits, and now as an entrepreneur. The sunflower blossomed in every situation and profession. I was open and loyal and full of vibrance. Now, as I lead my two businesses as a mental health provider, author, podcaster, speaker, community healer, and consultant, I am fully embracing my power and the transferable skills that I obtained on my own.

When I gave birth to my first business, it was to bring together social work leaders in different industries who have been healing and inspiring communities. Really, Latinx in Social Work Inc. is more than a business; it is a revolution. We publish English/Spanish anthologies of personal essays written by Latinx/e social workers, giving them the space to share what drove them to social work and how being Latinx/e has shaped their experience.

Now two volumes in with a third on the way, these books help readers feel less alone, validating their experiences of discrimination, celebrating their presence in our profession, and building community. *Latinx/e in Social Work* is also used in social work school curricula to educate about the urgent need for culturally humble social workers. Additionally, the series provides tangible support to the next generation of Latinx/e social workers because we donate all retail proceeds to the Latino Social Work Coalition and Scholarship Fund, reducing the financial burden of pursuing social work and increasing the number of Latinx/e who are able to follow their dreams of becoming social workers. We're challenging the status quo and striving to build a social work future that looks like the communities we serve. Our communities need us to heal and be well.

I gave birth to my second business, Sandoval Psychotherapy Consultation LCSW PLLC, shortly after the first. Also known as Sandoval CoLab, this is the bread and butter of my work, and notably, where my income is generated. On one side, I operate a therapy practice, overseeing a team of all-women, majority-Latina clinicians who are culturally humble and trauma informed. The other half of the business is hosting trainings about mental health, wellness, and diversity, equity, and inclusion. We lead trainings for corporations, nonprofits, schools, families, and other mental health providers.

Today, I'm in the process of giving birth to my third business. It focuses on the healing journey through psychedelics. As a certified ketamine-assisted clinical therapist, I have seen and experienced the greatest power of healing: knowing.

In my psychedelic journeys, I have seen sunflowers, horses, birch trees. Loyalty, strength, rebirth. I have learned about myself and the strengths of my gifts. This has been key to being a successful business owner. I want to bring this back to our communities and support trauma healing. Indigenous ancestors have done this for centuries, and I'm reclaiming it.

Being a Latina business owner has not been easy, but it has been rewarding. I have a sense of freedom and extreme pride. I was not the first entrepreneur in my family. I have ancestors who have done this before. I often remember this quote from Isaac Newton, "If I have seen further, it is by standing on the shoulders of giants."

I am not the first, and I learned from many. Now we hope you can take a page out of our book and learn from us. You are not alone.

My Final Business Diva Word:

BEGIN

ABOUT ERICA PRISCILLA SANDOVAL

Erica Priscilla Sandoval is an award-winning mental health practitioner, public speaker, executive coach, entrepreneur, podcaster, philanthropist, and author of *Latinx/e in Social Work Volumes I and II.* She is also the founder and CEO of Sandoval Psychotherapy Consulting—known as Sandoval CoLab—where she oversees a team of social workers and leads mental health, wellness, and diversity, equity, and inclusion work for organizations, universities, health care facilities, medical, and corporate professionals.

Erica began her career in the music industry before pivoting to social work, which led to her spending seven years as an advocate for children and families at the New York City Hospital for Special Surgery and working at the Make-A-Wish Foundation. During the pandemic, Erica opened her own private therapy practice.

She holds an associate's degree from the Borough of Manhattan Community College, a bachelor's degree from Baruch College, and a master's in social work from the New York University Silver School of Social Work. She is also trained in Ketamine-Assisted Psychotherapy (KAP), a breakthrough approach to an awakened mind and healing trauma and depression. Erica was recently named New York Socia of Latina Empire, a personal and business development coaching program.

The recipient of many awards, Erica was recognized by Prospanica-NY with the 2021 Top Latinx Leaders, Social

Justice award, and the Make-A-Wish Foundation gave Erica the 2018 Diversity and Inclusion Innovation Award.

She was a contributing author to *Today's Inspired Latina, Volume X*, and *Latinx/e in Social Work*, and received an honorable mention at the 24th annual International Latino Book and Film Awards. In 2020, Erica became the first immigrant Latina president of the National Association of Social Workers' New York City chapter and is now the chapter's President Emeritus.

Erica is a philanthropist and is a donor to the Latino Social Work Coalition and Scholarship Fund. Erica was most recently recognized as a Latino Leader on the radar by Latino Leaders in Action.

As a proud immigrant from Ecuador, her passion is fueled by supporting the community she is a part of and their children. Her greatest pride is being a single mother and raising her twenty-two-year-old daughter, Isabella, whom she considers her biggest teacher.

Erica Priscilla Sandoval, LCSW-SIFI
latinxinsocialwork.com
IG: latinxinsocialwork
LinkedIn: Erica Priscilla Sandoval, LCSW
sandovalcolab.com
IG: sandovalcolab

An Entrepreneur at Heart: Following My Calling to Serve Others

JACQUELINE S. RUIZ

"Entrepreneurship is the only way to abundance. Be your own boss." —Jesus Camacho

I vividly remember those words from my dad. He instilled the idea of entrepreneurship from an early age. He had been an entrepreneur in multiple businesses since he had to grow really quickly after his dad passed away at a young age. His creativity, work ethic, and his desire to serve the community led to his hardworking journey in various states throughout Mexico.

As I saw my dad manage several businesses, my mother began to work at various multi-level marketing companies, which, in essence, are running your own business with some guidance. I was the only girl and the youngest, and would be with my mother most of the time. Her new ventures were filled with inspiring business books provided by the companies she was associated with.

As these two pathways joined from my dad's business acumen to my mom's newfound passion for business books, I was curious about how I could eventually build my own. Authors like Zig Ziglar, Napoleon Hill, Og Mandino, and Dale Carnegie began to shape what would become my entrepreneurship journey. My quest was augmented by the few years that we lived in what was, at the time, one of the biggest cities in the world in terms of population: Mexico City. Living in the hustle and bustle of a big city opened my eyes to the window to the world.

Unfortunately, at seven years old, my parents decided to move to a town with only six thousand people. My dreams of entrepreneurship seemed to have been crushed at the time, since I thought the town would not be big enough for my big aspirations. I would often feel like I was asphyxiating there, not only because it was so small, but because of the mindset of people that lived there. Often misunderstood for my high energy and overachiever attitude, every day that I was living there seemed to take my dream of entrepreneurship and abundance further and further away from me.

While I was living in this situation, my only "escape" would be books. I began devouring the golden lessons these books contained, taking notes, reading, rereading passages, asking questions about what they meant, and making them part of my life, until one day...something catastrophic happened. Someone ignited a fire in our house in the small town we lived in.

To our dismay, 80 percent of the books that I read were burned. It was what would become the first devastating moment of my life, but something inside of me made me feel a ray of light: hope. I knew that I had studied, analyzed, and embraced the lessons in those books, so now it was up to me to use those lessons in my endeavor as an entrepreneur. The only issue was that I was only twelve years old at that time. I was an entrepreneur waiting to happen.

My big break happened after my parents decided to immigrate to the United States when I was fourteen years old. Now I had a big enough space to create my big dreams: the land of dreams! I had heard so many stories of money growing on trees in the United States and how there were opportunities for everyone that worked hard. I knew that I was a hardworking, dedicated person, which, combined with the lessons from the books, would potentially give me all the ingredients needed to achieve the "American Dream."

As I adapted to my life in the United States, I started to feel frustration and confusion. People were talking, communicating, and exchanging information, but I could not understand anything they were saying. I loved talking to people and learning about their stories, but not speaking English created a big gap in my dream. I knew that I had to learn the language first to understand how business was done in this country. I had to focus all of my energy on learning the grammatical structure of a sentence and then memorize the meaning, use, and pronunciation of the words for me to become bilingual.

There were times that I thought it was impossible. Every time I fully understood a concept, it would change in the next sentence. The English language indeed has some weird rules! The back of shampoo bottles, advertisements, an old notebook, and a pen were my best friends. I would often listen to TV and radio in English before I went to sleep. I read that these actions would help you accelerate the process.

I felt lost, confused, and oftentimes incapable of learning any new English until I got my break...something started to shift. I started thinking and even dreaming in English. I thought I was going crazy! I told my mother about this and she could not believe it. She told me that it was a sign that I was becoming bilingual!

Immediately, I started feeling a bit more confident. Sometimes you don't realize how far you've come in your journey until someone that loves you reminds you of your accomplishments. Thank you, Mom, for putting things into perspective. This newly found confidence let me start taking German in English, and later becoming a German tutor. I knew that pushing myself to the next level of learning a completely different language in English would perhaps confuse me at first, but in the long run, helped me master the English language faster.

There was a new perspective for me after my mom told me that. I felt hope that I could finally take the next step into becoming the entrepreneur that I was meant to be; however, many more years would pass before taking the leap of faith to create my first company. Even though I could communicate now in English, I had no idea what my talents were that could be translated into a business that people would pay for. I had no experience, just still a dream waiting to happen.

At eighteen years old, right after I graduated with honors from high school, my dad left my mom and me. Instead of focusing on my education, I had to leave the community college that I started going to, to support my mother. My dream was put on hold again.

Always with gratitude in my heart regardless of the circumstances, I would have up to three jobs at a time to make ends meet for my mom and me. I worked in retail, hospitality, and restaurants, all with a twist of sales and a little bit of marketing.

Exactly nine years after my arrival in the United States, almost to the date, my dream of owning a business finally became a reality. At just twenty-three years old, I launched my first business: JJR Marketing, a full-service marketing/PR agency serving start-ups and small businesses. My boyfriend at the time gifted me my first ever laptop computer that would prove essential for my new endeavor. I married him and had my first child, which became the perfect opportunity to start my business, since I did not want to work long hours with the baby anymore. My husband had a steady job with great health benefits, and that safety net allowed me to take the leap of faith into the unknown.

I started connecting with my network, attending events, and following up with previous contacts to launch my business. I was a one-woman show for the first couple of years, locking myself up in my room while my mother took care of my little baby. I would come out of my room to take breaks just as if I were in a job, being disciplined in every way I could.

My first client was an Indian restaurant located a few

miles away from my house. They hired me in the first meeting because apparently, they had heard wonderful things about my work ethic and had been looking for me (while I was on maternity leave) to help them with their marketing. They were a godsend, not only because they trusted in me first, but because while I was there, I ate a spice that day that ended up saving my life! That story in itself is a miracle, and you can find it in my memoir, *The Fig Factor*, published in 2013.

I continued my business for many years, primarily serving the hospitality industry doing campaigns, public relations, and website updates, until I had one chance to do the marketing for an IT company. This small opportunity back in 2010 turned out to be one of the biggest blessings of my new business. The recession hit the restaurant industry the hardest in 2008, just two years after I started the business, resulting in me losing a big percentage of my clients that closed down. The opportunity to work with less volatile industries proved to be one of the best decisions that would carry our growth forward.

My husband started to see that this small business could be something. He saw my frustration with my freelance graphic designer missing the mark again and again on a brochure for a doctor that I had been hired to do. While on his winter break from his job, he saw an opportunity to self-learn the design applications overnight and produced the most stunning brochure the next day. I presented the newly redesigned brochure by my husband to the doctor and she loved it!

From there, he started sharing his amazing talent to create more stunning designs for my other clients, and it caught on. He eventually left his job to work with me full-time. We were a match made in heaven, not only in life, but now in business too. That year we grew 56 percent with this new addition!

For a while, we continued to work with our clients and one freelance writer. Between the three of us, we represented what every client would need: content, design, and strategy/management. It then became obvious that we needed to grow. I brought in my first few employees, but since I had no experience in a professional agency, I had no idea that I needed to delegate. My frustrations began to grow, and I ended up firing my first employee. It was the most difficult day of my life. Many months went by and I had not found someone that could help understand the process and replicate it, until I found it in the least expected place: an intern.

All of a sudden, this intern would anticipate problems and solve them, and would proactively document and prepare items for meetings ahead of time. I could not believe it! I had found my person! I eventually hired her to implement systems and processes augmented by technology that allowed me to grow to sixteen collaborators in just a year.

In 2020, I joined a very small number of female entrepreneurs with over $1M in revenue that represent only 2.6% percent of women-owned businesses for the first time in my journey. This challenge to make it over the six figures came from the desire to be accepted at a prestigious accelerator program at Stanford University called Stanford Latino Entrepreneurship Initiative. I worked hard with our team to make it happen in the middle of the pandemic, and it worked!

I am now a consultant to many multimillion-dollar companies across the United States and Puerto Rico thanks to this amazing program that opened my horizon to share my talent of strategy with others. Now with two successful award-winning businesses, I feel more connected to my mission than ever. **After all, it is all about service.**

My biggest tips for women starting their businesses are the following:

- Start with gratitude.
- Package up your experience and knowledge for the service of others, always.
- Capture and document your small "wins" to help you during difficult times.
- It's never about the money. The money comes in abundance when you become a dream catcher for others.

My Final Business Diva Word:

MAGIX (magic x 10)

Entrepreneurship is one of the most amazing pathways to abundance and to achieving your dreams. Remember to be grounded in your values, activate your talents, and land on your dreams.

ABOUT JACQUELINE RUIZ

Jacqueline Ruiz is a visionary social entrepreneur that has created an enterprise of inspiration. With twenty years of experience in the marketing and public relations industry, she has created two successful award-winning companies, established two nonprofit organizations, published twenty-nine books, created many products, and held dozens of events around the world. She has received over thirty awards for her business acumen.

Jacqueline is currently the CEO of JJR Marketing, one of the fastest-growing top marketing and public relations agencies in Chicago, and Fig Factor Media, a media publishing company that helps individuals bring their books to life. Jacqueline is also the Founder of The Fig Factor Foundation, a nonprofit organization dedicated to giving vision, direction, and structure to young Latinas, as well as the President of Instituto Desarrollo Amazing Aguascalientes, the first youth center in Calvillo, Aguascalientes, Mexico.

Jacqueline currently serves as a board member for the World Leaders Forum, The Fig Factor Foundation, LovePurse, and the Alumni Executive Board at the College of DuPage. She is a recent graduate of the Stanford University Latino Business Action Network, and the Women Entrepreneurship Cohort 3 from DePaul University, among others. Jacqueline is one of the few sports Latina airplane pilots in the United States.

Jacqueline Ruiz
jackie@jjrmarketing.com
IG: @pilotina_official
LinkedIn: Jacqueline Camacho-Ruiz

LIFE'S PIVOTAL MOMENTS

JOANN P. ORNELAS-BAUER

"Moments of clarity provide us with new perspectives and opportunities to change our lives."

THE CALL

It was August 1, 2016, and I was preparing for my trip to San Diego, California, to accept a job, when a call came in from a former coworker, asking for a few minutes of my time to pitch a business opportunity. After about twenty minutes of him spilling out his ideas, I was intrigued by the thought of owning and starting a business. I agreed that I would somehow postpone accepting the job and meet him for breakfast the following Monday.

For the next several days, my thoughts and emotions ranged from the excitement of becoming an entrepreneur to fear of "what if it didn't work" to feeling guilty that I gave a verbal acceptance to a job offer and now I may not follow through. I finally convinced myself that I could buy enough time to make the best decision for my life's destiny.

Monday morning arrived, and I was extremely nervous. My mind raced all night, thinking of what the meeting would be like. Could it be a waste of our time? What if we fail before we start? Did I make the wrong decision not to formally accept the job offer? I know my "now" business partner was just as nervous, as this was his second attempt to find a business partner.

We met at a café in Elmhurst, Illinois. He brought another person to this meeting, which was a surprise to me, as I felt I was being tag-teamed. They both had plenty to say about this opportunity, and they made things sound so simple and exciting—demand for diverse suppliers, my experience was a perfect fit, utilizing our experience to make a difference in the electric utility industry, the business structure was easy to set up, and so on and so on.

My head was spinning during that meeting and for days after. I had so much to reconcile in my mind, but I knew in my gut when I left breakfast that I had a chance to be part of something great. It would require a very quick and in-depth industry and business investigation to guide my decision, as this would be one of the biggest and riskiest decisions of my life.

I couldn't stall much longer, as I was getting pressure from the San Diego company to sign the job acceptance papers. I had to decide. Only ten days after our breakfast meeting, I decided to take the entrepreneurial path to cofound Dynamic (not yet named at the time).

Despite the huge risks—investing all that we worked for and owned—to start a construction company that builds the poles and wires to the electric grid, it was an opportunity of a lifetime that I knew would never come again. With the always-loving support of my husband, I was all in. At the age of fifty-three, I was giving up the safe, corporate world for a risky, entrepreneurial, make-it-your-own environment. Not to mention, it meant more deep-freezing Chicago winters.

It has been almost six years since Dynamic opened for business, and through the many ups (i.e., landing our first contract, which was short-lived) and downs (i.e., constantly feeding the capital beast of a business and not taking any pay for more than a year), and plenty of uncertainties (i.e., can we generate enough work to keep our employees employed and pay our debts?), I'm often asked, "Would you do it again?" I answer with an absolute YES, I'd do it again a million times over! I'm surrounded by the right partners, who have fought in the trenches with me. I know that the culmination of my life's experiences, learnings, and skills prepared me for this.

EARLY YEARS

I am the fourth of six kids born to Sally and Francisco Ornelas. Until the age of seven, my family of eight lived in a two-bedroom house in Wilmington, California, surrounded by family—grandparents, aunts, uncles, and cousins. My parents met and married young, and neither finished high school. As with any parent, their dream was to give us more opportunities than they had growing up. To them, that meant moving us out of Wilmington.

My dad would pack us all into our Volkswagen Bug on weekends and take us on long drives. My sister and I would climb into the "back hole" as we called it and wave to people as we passed them by. Today, my parents would be arrested for child endangerment—no car seats or seat belts, not to mention no bumper on the back of the VW bug.

One weekend, my dad found his way to Mission Viejo, California, which is about forty-five miles south of Wilmington. It was a booming town with lots of new housing tracks among the thousands of acres of orange groves. This community was way above what they could afford, but Dad was determined. It took some convincing from my mom to leave her family and friends, with whom we spent time almost every day visiting and playing.

We grew up in a time when assimilation was an emphasis. My parents chose not to have us speak Spanish in the home, despite it being their first language. They thought it would be better for assimilating into any community we moved to. Mom and Dad each worked two to three jobs to afford our new life of better opportunities.

LOW EXPECTATIONS FOR THE DOUBTERS

When I was young, I had dreams of becoming a teacher, a child psychologist, or a pediatrician. But others had different thoughts about the future for me. When I got to high school, I thought I'd be in classes with my friends, but my counselor placed me in remedial classes and told me I wasn't smart enough to be with them, and that I should become a secretary and find a husband and have a family. I shouldn't waste my time dreaming of things that I would never be capable of. This type of counseling continued into my community college days, where the counselor again told me I was wasting my time thinking about higher education.

Thank goodness the strength of my thoughts and dreams for myself overruled the doubters. I always heard a voice in my head and felt in my gut that I would do something big with my life. I didn't let the low expectations that others had for me interfere with the expectations I had for myself.

BELIEVING IN ME

While I received no help to prepare for college, I figured it out myself. I had no idea what going to a university would be like, but thought that if I could just get into a university, I'd be okay.

Boy, was I in for a shock. I was not prepared, as I don't think that my reading and writing skills were even at a ninth-grade level. I had never written an essay, let alone a term paper. I was scared that I would fail and be kicked out, and my dream of a college degree would vanish. I signed up for two writing classes, which meant I had a writing assignment every day. I struggled throughout my bachelor's program, but I graduated, barely, and received my degree.

Developing good writing skills has greatly contributed to my successful career throughout the years. Writing was my foundational skill upon which many more skills were built upon. Writing is a great form of communication.

NONTRADITIONAL CAREER

After receiving my bachelor's degree, I landed a job with the state of California as a hazardous waste specialist. It was my introduction to construction. There were not a lot of women in this field, let alone Mexican Americans. I had a hunger to learn as much as possible, and volunteered to take on any project to ensure I built new skills.

I later was hired into an engineering and construction company, where I had the opportunity to expand my skill set as well as travel the US and South Pacific. After years of traveling, I decided it was time for a career change to learn and experience something new. I was advised that I would need a higher degree, a master's. Again, I was met with doubters, even after more than ten years with an established career. I was told that I wasn't smart enough. I still applied, and was accepted to the Pepperdine University master's in business program.

This time, I finished my degree with an A- grade point average. The skills I developed through the years paid off. I landed a job with an electric utility company in Chicago, IL, and made the drastic move from Southern California.

Today, in the US, few electric utility construction companies are founded and owned by minority women. While there are many barriers to becoming an entrepreneur, it's not impossible to make your dream come true. I attribute my success to tuning out the doubters, my relentless pursuit of developing skills, being curious about learning and trying new things, and finding strong partners that believed in me.

LIFE'S PIVOTAL MOMENTS

The many challenges I faced turned out to be blessings that brought me to where I am today. In life, we experience pivotal moments—moments of clarity that provide us with new perspectives and opportunities to change our lives. Reflecting on my life, some of the most impactful pivotal moments were 1) almost failing out of college—I became determined to build my skills; 2) my first career job—I was introduced to construction; 3) changing careers—I received an MBA and joined the electric utility industry; and 4) co-founding Dynamic—the greatest challenge and greatest reward, and I'd do it again, a million times over. And of course, meeting and marrying my husband of eighteen years is my greatest pivotal moment. He's my biggest fan and my life partner who has supported me every step of the way.

I've always had dreams of having my own business, and once I did set up a consulting company, but it was short-lived, and I found myself back in the safety of the corporate world. My corporate experience, ability to invest and save, and my acquired toolbox of skills put me in a position for an even bigger dream to become a reality. What young girl grows up thinking "I want to build power lines"? It certainly wasn't me, but my dream of becoming an entrepreneur and business owner is bigger and better than I ever imagined. While some think I'm just lucky, it was a lifetime of preparing for the opportunities presented to me.

My determination to tune out the doubters and guide my own destiny allowed me to be open to opportunities that would teach me new skills, which in turn created more opportunities.

51

My Final Business Diva Word:

RESILIENCE

Toughness; the ability to respond to change or adversity and the capacity to recover quickly from difficulties.

ABOUT JOANN P. ORNELAS-BAUER

In 2016, Ms. Ornelas-Bauer cofounded Dynamic Utility Solutions, an electric utility construction contracting company in Carol Stream, Illinois, and is a majority owner and CEO. Dynamic is a diverse supplier, holding both minority- and woman-owned business enterprises certificates. Dynamic provides IBEW labor services to build the poles and wires of the electric distribution system in Illinois. Dynamic also responds to storm restoration across the country.

Starting with seven employees and six trucks, Dynamic has grown to more than 110 employees with multiple departmental disciplines and a full fleet of utility vehicles and equipment.

Construction itself is a nontraditional career path for a Mexican American woman. After receiving her bachelor's degree in biology, she landed her first career job as a hazardous waste specialist in California. It was the start of her lifelong career in construction. She went on to receive her master's in business and has been in the electric utility industry for more than twenty years.

She grew up in Southern California and moved to Chicago, Illinois, in 2000. She is married and shares the hobbies of running ultra-marathons and tasting fine wines with her husband, Chris.

To advance opportunities in minority communities, Ms. Ornelas-Bauer serves as a board member of El Valor in Chicago, Illinois, and the Aurora Hispanic Chamber of Commerce in Illinois and is a member of HACIA (Hispanic American Construction Industry Association).

Joann Ornelas-Bauer

Cofounder and CEO for Dynamic Utility Solutions
Jbauer@dynamicusllc.com
LinkedIn: https://www.linkedin.com/feed/

ANA BUILES, MSN, FNP-C

"You're braver than you believe, stronger than you see, and smarter than you think." —A.A. Milne

Since I was a young girl, I always knew I wanted to make a difference—and I have always been intrigued by the medical field.

My father and grandfather always believed females should excel and accomplish their goals. My grandfather came from Colombia to New York City with not a lot of money, and worked really hard to bring his entire family legally to the United States of America.

My grandfather wanted a promising future for his family. He did not have a college degree, but became successful in the real estate profession. Having this upbringing and seeing how hard my grandfather and father worked to provide for the family encouraged me to think big about my goals.

I have always wanted to be a boss, a leader, and the owner of my own medical practice, but I did not know how to accomplish it or what area I wanted to specialize in. Throughout the years, I have learned of the law of attraction. As I worked hard and stayed positive, things started to fall into place.

After my father and grandfather's passing, I decided to pursue all my goals and not be afraid of any obstacles that would come my way during my journey. I wanted to make my loved ones proud of me, and I also wanted to prove to myself that I am a strong, confident woman who is not afraid of taking risks and chances in life.

I became a family nurse practitioner and had been practicing for the last three years. Before becoming a nurse practitioner, I was a registered nurse for nine years. Being in the nursing career for the previous twelve years of my life, I have learned that my passion has always been helping people feel their best. I have always had an interest in aesthetics.

More than two years ago, I decided to take the opportunity to learn medical aesthetics. I first researched which class to take, and I decided to take a beginner's injector course held in Manhattan, New York. After taking the course, I became even more interested in medical aesthetics and began my research in taking more educational courses and how to succeed as an aesthetic injector.

Then the covid pandemic shutdown happened; however, it did not stop me from learning. During the shutdown, I was taking webinars and doing more research in medical aesthetics. During all the research and webinars I took, I realized how passionate I am about medical aesthetics. I knew it would be a long journey, but nothing great comes from doing things the easy way. I knew that I would find my way into the medical aesthetic industry with perseverance. As an aesthetic injector, I believe in naturally enhancing one's beauty to build confidence. And since I have always loved and appreciated art, I can incorporate art with medicine in medical aesthetics.

I have applied to various medical aesthetics spas for an aesthetic injector job position, but did not get a response from the companies, so I decided to take the matter into my own hands and work as an aesthetic injector doing home concierge services with my friends, family, and coworkers.

After working for a few months doing home concierge services, I started to post my aesthetic work on social media. During the process of me doing concierge services and working on my social media skills, I had a medical spa located in Manhattan, New York, reach out to me for an interview. I was offered a part-time job within the medical spa.

While I was working at the medical spa, I was able to interact with different individuals. I worked in the medical spa for a few months, and during those months, I learned and developed advanced injection skills. The more practice and training I received, the better I got at assessing individual facial anatomy. While working part-time at the medical spa in Manhattan and full-time as a nurse practitioner at New York Presbyterian, I was still working on my home concierge business.

I am very grateful for the opportunity the medical spa gave me; however, I wanted to focus more on my business.

I decided to name my medical aesthetic practice Just Glam Medical Aesthetics. During this time of my life, I have learned many life lessons. Perseverance and commitment are the keys to overcoming any obstacles.

There were moments when I had to overcome negative thoughts because my life had become extremely busy. I was juggling my personal and work life, which became a struggle. There were nights when I would cry and just wanted to quit on everything because my time management with my personal and work life had become very intense. However, my drive and passion for medical aesthetics kept me going whenever I felt those thoughts come to me. I kept reminding myself that all this was temporary and that I would be rewarded in the end.

Throughout my aesthetic injector journey, I have met and trained with various master injectors around the country. I believe in continuing education because aesthetic medicine keeps evolving. I also developed good networking with a handful of local aesthetic injectors whom I became friends with. It is essential to have excellent networking within your career, because that is where you will find great mentors that will guide you in any roadblocks you will have during your goal journey.

I usually keep in touch with my mentors in many ways, such as via social media, email, and phone calls. Social media has become imperative for marketing proposes for all entrepreneurs, and it may be a struggle for some individuals who need to be social media savvy. I was never social media savvy; however, I did my research like with medical aesthetics and received guidance from social media gurus.

Over the past two years and more, I had many hats in my medical aesthetics practice, such as receptionist, booking, inventory, marketing for social media, interior designer, aesthetic injector, and medical director. Being on my own has been very challenging, but also very rewarding. Having so many responsibilities, I learned different aspects of this profession and reminded myself that I started this incredible journey because of my passion for medical aesthetics.

Going through these different emotions and obstacles and having so many hats, I appreciated medical aesthetics more and became an entrepreneur.

I used to be very insecure about my decisions in life. I always questioned myself on every decision I would take, and even worse, I was always very indecisive. With my passion growing for medical aesthetics and becoming an entrepreneur, I became more confident in my decisions. I could see my ideas more clearly and execute them without thinking twice. I also learned through my mistakes; that is how I got better as an aesthetic injector and as an entrepreneur.

As a woman from a Hispanic background, I faced many challenges. However, being a minority, female, and the firstborn of my siblings made me stronger, and I desired to inspire individuals like me who want to become female entrepreneurs.

I had many doors that were closed on me; along the road, I had some individuals who doubted me when searching for an aesthetic job. They thought I was ridiculous for starting a new passion after being in the medical field for about ten years; however, that obstacle did not stop me from pursuing my aspirations in the medical aesthetic field. It made me courageous to keep going and not give up on my goals because owning a business, especially a medical aesthetic practice, comes with a significant commitment.

I decided to part ways at the medical spa I worked with for a few months to dedicate more time to medical aesthetic practice. That said, I only focused on my full-time job as a nurse practitioner at New York Presbyterian, and my other days for my medical aesthetic practice. As I made more moves in my medical practice by getting more advanced training and developing more patients, I finally opened a Just Glam Medical Aesthetics location in Astoria, New York.

Opening my business in a location has been a tremendous accomplishment. I never gave up during the process, and I firmly believed what I had to bring to the industry was special. Having this drive made me become who I am today, and I know I still have much work. Just Glam Medical Aesthetics has been open since early February 2022, and my patients have increased since February.

Being a medical business owner definitely comes with a lot of commitment, risky decisions, and many hats in the beginning, but most importantly, believe in yourself. As a small business owner, I have learned that believing in myself and the goals I wanted to accomplish have genuinely made me come so far and become more knowledgeable in the medical aesthetic industry.

Remember that there is always room to make mistakes because that is how I have learned to grow as an entrepreneur; I'm still growing within medical aesthetics because you never stop learning. New challenges will arise every day, but always remember that there are answers to every challenge. I see entrepreneurship as a marathon, mind over matter. It may seem like the road is long, but there is always a finishing line with a reward. Whatever goals I set, I know that with a lot of work and dedication, they will eventually be accomplished. Do not ever be afraid to ask for guidance; I would not be here today if it weren't for my aesthetic mentors, other small business owners, family, and friends.

My Final Business Diva Word:

FEARLESS

The one word that keeps coming up in my mind for my readers is fearless. The word fearless has many symbolic synonyms that define a strong woman, such as courageous, bold, and brave on any obstacles you face, while confident in making all the decisions you will come across. Being in the medical aesthetic industry and owning a medical aesthetic practice has made me fearless. Be brave in accepting any obstacles that come on your path, taking any mistakes, and learning from them. Stand up for what you believe in.

As a woman entrepreneur, you will face many challenges, but as a fearless individual, you will be able to face any obstacles. Having a fearless attitude will aid you in overcoming any bumps on your path to success. As a fearless entrepreneur, you will be okay with disappointments or failures because you know you will learn from them, which will not stop you from achieving your goal. Being fearless, you would not worry about any competition because you know your worth and have a lot to bring to the table of whichever business aspirations you have in mind. Fearless is not being proud and understanding that it is okay to take advice from another colleague. Being fearless, you can make a difference as a leader.

As an entrepreneur, you will become a leader within your community and guide aspiring individuals in their endeavors. And that is exactly what I want to do; as I keep learning to improve myself as a leader every day, I eventually would like to train and educate aspiring injectors on how to become great leaders in the medical aesthetics field. There is room for growth for every individual who aspires to become a leader in their specialty. Remember to be fearless and persevere, and you will achieve your goals.

ABOUT ANA BUILES

Ana Builes is a Family Nurse Practitioner with over three years of experience and twelve years as a registered nurse. Her specialties are Neonatal Health, Perioperative, Women's Health, and Medical Aesthetics. Ana got involved in medical aesthetics over two years ago and fell in love with it. Ana's passion has always been helping others feel their best, and she can now do so as she incorporates her artistic eye into the aesthetic industry. Being an aesthetic injector, she can combine medicine and art.

She has an extensive medical background in perioperative and is very knowledgeable regarding medical procedures. Ana has trained with master injectors around the country and believes in continuing her education because aesthetic medicine is constantly evolving. She started in Just Glam Medical Aesthetics as a home concierge service, but she had the vision to start her own medical practice. Just Glam Medical Aesthetics has a home now in the heart of Astoria, New York. Her business provides neurotoxin, facial contouring with dermal fillers and biostimulators, body contouring, IV therapy, and skin care. Ana strives to help her patients feel beautiful and confident by incorporating medicine and art. Your face is her canvas!

Ana Builes, MSN, FNP-C
Justglamaesthetics@gmail.com
IG: Injector_ana

DR. ALICIA E. LA HOZ

"Lead yourself first to catalyze the growth of others from a place of health."

Within six hours on a Thursday afternoon, I received news from two different sources of cuts of close to one million dollars. On the phone with our COO, overlooking the Washington, DC monuments in the hotel, we cringed at the decisions that had to be made.

By the following Tuesday, we had dismissed stellar staff. We notified organizations we supported to run programs of the funding cuts. I felt like I was betraying the trust of dedicated people. Were we really one of those organizations that had shown up in at risk-communities and fanned the flames of hope and passion, only to turn away and leave? It was a painful process that heightened the need of diversifying our funding model.

BREAKING THROUGH STRUCTURAL ROADBLOCKS

As a clinical psychologist seeing firsthand the consequences of shattered relationships, I founded and directed Family Bridges, a nonprofit, seventeen years ago to help end the cycle of family trauma through innovative programs that empower, encourage, and equip individuals in low-income communities.

For the first fifteen years, we were mostly funded by philanthropic and public grants, including $30 million in federal grants. We had given away $14 million in a shared revenue model to up to twenty-two other providers. Together, we delivered comprehensive programs to over 150,000 individuals and families. We provided training, background support, evaluation, and resources, and innovated, expanding our programs from face-to-face support to reaching an audience with multimedia assets. Our online, radio, and theater experiences and our citywide approach expanded our reach from the Chicagoland area to multiple states and to Latin America.

The collective impact model opened doors to correctional facilities, substance abuse centers, medical centers, churches, schools, and community centers—we could go beyond the walls and reach Latinos everywhere they were.

As we approached our second funding cycle and garnered national attention, the question keeping me up at night was "How can we bring these exceptional programs to scale?" Providers, volunteers, and facilitators at the table carried the scars and mended hearts of Latinos, reaching them like a quilted blanket. Witnessing people change and moving forward in a collective impact approach was energizing, and we wanted to do more and go further.

"A nonprofit is a business." The speaker's words grabbed my attention and started me on a journey to discover what this meant. Of course, it made great sense. Nonprofit businesses require governance, marketing and sales, talent development, risk management, financial controls, and strategic direction. People, product(s), and processes are integral to both organizational structures.

I led book clubs with our staff and board and learned about disciplined thought, disciplined people, and disciplined action, and the five levels of executive leadership from Jim Collins in his best-seller, *Good to Great.* We learned from *Forces for Good: The Six Practices of High-Impact Nonprofits* by Leslie Crutchfield and Heather Grant, about the value of harnessing market forces and leveraging business partners within the nonprofit work. I leaned heavily on our COO, Omaira Gonzalez, and we were engrossed in building an executive team and investing in a culture of servant leadership within our organization—one that would truly live out the values we espoused.

We held strategic retreats, put together a multidisciplinary advisory board, studied expansion models, sought counsel from other successful ventures, and strategized and tested business plans.

As we embraced a servant leadership approach, Bridges XL was formed in 2019 as an LCC. We received multiple inquiries and contracts to provide leadership development and relationship education as a wellness initiative given the spill-over effects of family well-being impacting productivity and efficiency in the workplace. We created the Four C's of leadership (Clarity, Communication, Creativity, Culture) modules and delivered these to C-level executives of a Fortune 500 health care organization and business leaders across industries. Additionally, we positioned Bridges XL as a business where at least 10 percent of the funds generated would be donated to Family Bridges to support its operations, helping to diversify the nonprofit's source of support.

A TURNING POINT

After listening to a philanthropic leader share an impactful chart depicting the $485 billion annually given in charitable care to 1.54 million charities in the US compared to the 20 trillion available in the marketplace, the numbers spoke through the noise. Thanks to God's favor, I was part of the 1 percent of Latino-led nonprofits that had received big bets in philanthropic and federal dollars to run charitable work. Would we continue to fight for these restricted funds exclusively, or would we venture out and expand our funding source to unrestricted funds in the marketplace?

We entered a season of creative destruction to focus on building a more diverse funding model. Right before the pandemic, we stopped pursuing funding for the same type of programs we had learned to depend on over the years. Instead, we limited development to strategic initiatives only and focused our attention on pursuing impact investment. Even when we received rejections on projects proposed, we leaned forward. Remarkably, amid COVID, our executive team leaned in, volunteering to keep the operations and organization afloat. They demonstrated an unsurpassed passion, dedication, and support that lifted me and encouraged me to give it all I had.

CASADEMIA IS BORN

Years of content development meant we had built an impressive catalog of content geared toward the Latino community. Casademia was born as an e-Learning platform featuring Family Bridges research-based family strengthening curricula and BridgesXL coaching and leadership programs.

Casademia provides an opportunity to bring high-quality family and relationship programming to Hispanic families under a hybrid model of face-to-face engagement with online support. By partnering with churches and coaches in local communities under a profit-sharing model, our programs can scale. Casademia's profit-sharing model seeks to compensate community coaches for their time, offering a sustainable solution for social impact.

DEFINING OUR NICHE

Mental health, relationship well-being, and leadership are all passions that have occupied different spaces in my life: clinical practice, family strengthening, leadership, and coaching.

Women in leadership are at the intersection of these three passions. Women are at the helm of making decisions at home, in business, as board members, and in ministry. They are rubbing shoulders with mental health concerns, and they are working through relational conflicts day in and day out. And in these roles, all three of these areas come to play.

Thus, as I led our team in implementing the Casademia model, our focus turned to the decision-makers in our midst. Who is running homes and businesses? Latinas in leadership are found in educational, business, and civic life, and are making a footprint in more ways than one in their spheres of influence. So, as we fine-tune our business model, we are focused on building the Casademia group coaching model with Latinas in leadership.

SUCCEEDING BOTH AT HOME AND IN BUSINESS

Over the years, I have listened to the aching hearts of Latina women either in clinical practice, business meetings, workshops, or business coaching groups. A common thread shared is the fear, shame, and insecurity they struggle with, which either keeps them silent, in abusive relationships, in less-than-ideal working environments, tolerating disrespect, and having enmeshed boundaries that have left them stretched.

Under pressure, many tolerate painful circumstances. Solace is often found in accepting that this lot and burden for them to carry is part of their *destino*. Like molten lava, however, years of pain have left a trace of bitterness and anger ready to erupt.

Latinas in leadership are rising like a silent army fighting this script. You may very well find yourself now in this company of resilient fighters. You have discovered opportunities where there were none and built and forged a path forward despite the rejections, setbacks, roadblocks, or barriers that came your way. You established boundaries. Each decision lifts you, helps you grow your confidence, and charts a path forward.

As the curtains are pulled, however, your one vulnerability may very well be at home. You may be struggling with motivating a child or spouse dealing with mental illness, grief, or struggling with addiction. You may be caring for an aging adult or working through a personal crisis. While you have conquered and succeeded in your public life, does it feel like your private life is shattered? Does it feel like you are blindly guiding others through a crisis?

Indeed, you want to succeed in both business and family life. You want to be valued for your contributions. You want to be taken seriously. You want to be listened to when you lean in. The problem is that you are juggling many demands, so it's easy to get lost in a sea of worry as you work through one conflict after another. As each situation leaves you second-guessing, you end up feeling depleted.

Ambivalence, insecurity, fear, and hopelessness are masters in crippling growth and crushing the spirit. They can derail and sap one's energy and strength. Wouldn't it be great if you could have a key to hijack your way out of problems and get on the other side in less time, with less worry and fretting? Imagine what it would mean to shed the weight and burden of insecurity, shame, and negative mindsets that creep their ugly head from time to time to pull you down. What if, instead of having a tight knot of emotional tension and a chaotic ensemble of competing thoughts dictating your restless sleep and feeding apprehension, you could have a way to sort through the pressure?

Imagine what it would mean not to have to be dragged down by the perpetual cycle of conflict that you may find yourself dancing with day in and day out with a spouse, a coworker, or family. What would it mean to unleash a method that could do just that? What would it mean to have a disciplined approach, a mental model to help iron out the wrinkled problems?

If we give this to Latina leaders, what would happen to their homes? What would happen to their businesses and ministry?

It is why my current focus is on our group coaching Casademia program that equips Latinas with the following:

1. A winning method that helps lift the daily pressure and lessen the load
2. Coaching to apply the method to current stressors
3. Tools to empower others in their leadership and/ or family so that they can take ownership of their struggles

By equipping Latinas with all of the above, many Latinas in leadership can stop feeling drained while navigating tension. As the battlefronts at home and in business are worn, Latinas can feel encouraged, emboldened, and empowered to give back and lead others from a place of health.

AN ANCHOR

As external and internal pressure takes its toll, it's easy to get carried away by negative thoughts that battle the mind, spirit, and body. Instead, my anchor in fighting the unsettling and shifting titans in my life has been to lean on Christ. He is my anchor, and in both the highs and lows, I have found that by being grounded in Him, I find peace and serenity to persevere. Knowing there is someone greater than me who has overcome the world and who is fighting the battles for me carries me above the fray. He gives me peace and holds me steady in the seasons of uncertainty and ambivalence. So, take heart and remember: He has overcome the world.

My Final Business Diva Word:

OVERCOMER

You are an overcomer. The tenacity, perseverance, fight, and hard work you pour into your home and work are remarkable. You have demonstrated resilience in overcoming adversity, disappointment, illness, pain, and loss. Adversity spurs you on and catalyzes you forward. You speak to others with a fire and passion that is fueled by years of experience because you are an overcomer.

ABOUT ALICIA E. LA HOZ

For twenty-three years, Alicia has brought psychological and social science research-based principles on mental health, leadership, professional development, and family life with a community-based approach. She obtained a doctorate in psychology from Wheaton College in 2004 and master's degree in counseling psychology from Trinity International University in 2001.

Alicia founded Family Bridges, a family-strengthening nonprofit organization operating in Chicago, Phoenix, and Portland, with affiliates in several Latin American cities. She expanded their imprint globally through a mini-drama series, *¡Qué Gente, Mi Gente!,* airing in twenty-six radio markets worldwide.

She also developed research-based curricula on conflict resolution and stress management with a trauma-informed approach based on outcomes of programs delivered to more than 165,000 people. She delivered professional development to key leaders and staff in a diversity of organizations, including Fortune 500 companies, leading to the formation of BridgesXL, which is focused on coaching and leadership development.

In 2013, Alicia authored the *Toolkit for Stakeholders Working with Latino Individuals, Couples and Families,* published by the National Resource Center for Healthy Marriage and Families and Romance Perpetuo, a resource workbook for Latino couples. In 2017, she co-authored *The Struggle Is Real: Modern Parenting,* a book and multimedia podcast.

74

For four years, she served on the Hispanic Research Work Group held by the Office of Planning, Research, and Evaluation within the Administration of Children and Families, US, HHS. Currently, she serves in the Family Life Board, a ministry of CRU.

Dr. Alicia E. La Hoz
www.familybridges.com

LEONOR GIL

"Fear Is A Reaction. Courage Is A Decision."
-Sir Winston Churchill

If you are an entrepreneur, you will never get any days off. That's what I would always hear. Growing up, I saw relatives enslaved in their businesses. I thought to myself, that's not something I ever want to do! I loved my free weekends and the structure, knowing that I would get a paycheck every two weeks.

For over thirty years, I grew accustomed to the same routine, the nine-to-five schedule, and the two to four weeks off a year allowed by my employer. I also enjoyed the benefits of having health, dental, and vision insurance at work.

I had not even contemplated becoming an entrepreneur. I was happy living the corporate life. My plans were to soon retire from my last employer. I had been doing well with my savings, profit sharing, and brokerage account, so I knew that in a few more years, I would get to retire comfortably.

Corporate life was not the best, but I was "living it" sometimes more stressful than others as politics played a big part. For the last thirty years of my life, I had spent it in different areas of finance. My first twenty were spent at a "top 10" investment management firm learning all about brokerage, client servicing, performance, management, billing, etc. The second part of my corporate experience was at a global custodian institution serving large corporations with all types of products.

The common denominator in those two phases of my career was that in both instances, I was supporting the growth of wealth for others, whether it be individual or institutional clients. I was helping them make more money. There is a saying in Spanish: *"Uno pone y Dios dispone"* which basically means One plans, and God decides. My grand plan, to stay with the company until retirement, came crashing down like a ton of bricks on my head.

One beautiful, snowy January morning I was called into a meeting with my manager. My manager and I had weekly update meetings. I was so happy prior to the meeting, as I had been preparing my list of updates. I had just been recognized for being the highest producer not just on my team, but the entire department. During this time, I was not looking forward to any type of monetary recognition. Although I had outperformed my peers and my expectations, I was not going to receive an increase in salary. Three years before this meeting, I was told I was making too much money and not only was my salary frozen, but my bonuses were also stopped.

I was not prepared for what was about to happen. This was the beginning of the Zoom era. I logged on to a meeting with two other individuals. I thought I was in the wrong meeting. As soon as my manager mentioned that the other person was an HR representative, I knew what was about to happen. My long-drawn-out plans of retiring with the corporation vanished as they announced that day would be my last day—actually the next fifteen minutes would be my last, not the entire day. I was not given the opportunity to say goodbye to my coworkers or even explain where I was in the process of pending items. All company and systems access were cut off in an instant. And just like that, I found myself out of a job.

NOW WHAT?

I was blessed to have been offered a small severance and outplacement assistance. I could easily start my next job search. Maybe it was the shock of what had just occurred or maybe it was the anger I felt being let go without notice. But I did not rush into finding my next opportunity. All my life, I had been limited to taking one to two weeks off at a time. This was my opportunity to take a break. I was idle for about a month. That didn't feel right, just enjoying days off, and no purpose in mind.

One of those days, a friend reached out asking how I was doing. In conversation, she reminded me of the opportunity to join WFG - World Financial Group as a business owner. A few years prior, I became a client and believed in the company's mission and products. One thing I recall learning that was very appealing was the opportunity to help families of all kinds of backgrounds. Up until now, I had been in the business of helping the wealthy get wealthier, and helping companies save more money. Here was an opportunity to help my family, my friends, and my community.

I had all the time in the world with no immediate plans to go back to a corporate job. For me to consider the entrepreneur route, I had to get yet another license. In my corporate life, I was able to secure several securities licenses. This one, however, would be as a life insurance producer. I knew nothing about the subject, but one thing I did know is that I wanted to learn and leave a legacy for my family—that has been one of my passions, to continually learn new things.

In a matter of weeks, I had studied and was ready to sit for the state examination. I was nervous, as I had not studied from notebooks nor tested in quite a few years. I believe in the power of visualization, so I put it to the test. I would visualize myself walking out of the testing center with a **PASS** report on hand...and so it happened! I was now a licensed producer in the state of Illinois, and it was then that my entrepreneur career began.

Not quite recuperated from the shock of being let go, I was still not quite ready to make a decision—should I look for another corporate position or become an entrepreneur? That was the question! As the days went on, I realized how burned out I felt. The last three years had been very stressful/difficult, losing my mom, becoming an empty nester, experiencing the worst health ever—my body was literally shutting down and moving from the house of twenty-seven years where I raised my kids.

The last few years raising my kids on my own had taught me to save for a rainy day. I had put away enough money to support myself for a few months. I had this grand idea to take advantage and once in my lifetime take an extended vacation—more than the customary two-week vacation. I decided to take an entire month off! Wow, that felt so good... So good, in fact, that the one month became three months!!

NEW PHASE IN MY LIFE

All good things come to end; it was back to reality! I had been avoiding the obvious decision: What do I do next? All my life in one shape or form I had been helping individuals, starting with my own family—translating Spanish to English, calling utility companies, making doctors' appointments, filling out applications, etc. It wasn't until I read *The Purpose-Driven Life* by Rick Warren that I realized what was my purpose in life...namely to be a servant leader.

That was the Aha! moment I needed to finally decide to become an entrepreneur. If I didn't give myself this opportunity, I was going to regret not taking a chance, I would say to myself as I pondered on the idea. So I took a leap of faith. I became a business owner, an entrepreneur.

No one ever said it was easy! Making the transition from a corporate employee to business owner mindset was challenging. I no longer had the nine-to-five schedule, I had to create my own, I no longer had the resources of an IT department, compliance area, human resources. I no longer had a structured job description to perform.

Looking back, I can honestly say that if it had not been for my thirty-plus years of experience in corporate doing multiple roles, it would have been a lot more difficult for me to make the transition. It was as if God had been preparing me all those years to handle every aspect of being a business owner.

My mom used to tell me, "If you're going to tackle something, do it right, otherwise don't do it!" I lived by this mantra, whether it was doing dishes, washing clothes, or learning a new job. This time it was no different.

I dived into learning as much as I could any given day. I was now responsible for creating my own schedule, making appointments, following up with clients, submitting new business, marketing myself, etc. The eight-hour days turned into twelve-hour days and a seven-day work week.

The best part about my new role as a business owner was the impact I was making, starting with my own family and friends. They now had someone they trusted as a go-to for anything finance related. This was the most gratifying part of my new life as an entrepreneur.

As with any new role, there are phases to be lived: the novelty phase, learning all new things; the adaptation, when I almost quit my new role; the realization that change is not easy; and the materialization phase, when I embraced my new role. Making the transition from corporate to entrepreneurship was definitely not easy.

The first several months were the most difficult. I had no schedule, no structure, no boss, etc. I felt a bit lost—more like a fish out of water and drowning at the same time. These first couple of months tested my resilience and patience and forced me to look inwards. Who am I? Why am I doing this?

Was I cut out to be an entrepreneur? There were days when I questioned whether I had made the right decision.

As humans, we tend to overthink things, when in reality, God is the one who is in control. What I mean is that change is not easy. However, when you surrender to God's will, everything makes sense.

One day, I suddenly stopped in the midst of my day when I realized what was happening. That was a huge revelation: During the past thirty years, I had been performing several roles, including administration, compliance, client services, technology, product knowledge, etc. Little did I know that all these years, God had been preparing me for this role—I was utilizing all that experience and skills accumulated over the years. This epiphany took over my soul, bringing me peace in the decision I had made, namely that the decision to become an entrepreneur was the correct one.

It has been over a year since I started this new phase of my life. The biggest opportunity I have as a business owner is the impact that I am making in the lives of others. Through my work, I am helping families with their finances. My goal is that through education, clients will pass on this knowledge to their children and grandchildren to finally break the poverty cycle and the scarcity mindset that has plagued us for such a long time.

In this past year, my confidence level has increased substantially. I am no longer afraid of failure. It is through failures that we learn and develop our skills while growing. I have earned the respect and trust of my peers and my clients. I continue to elevate others along my journey while providing education to make wise decisions about their finances.

My Final Business Diva Word:

COURAGE

Courage is the ability to do something that frightens you. Looking back, I realized I was afraid to start a new venture—after all, I was not a young woman anymore. I was afraid of failure, and what people, especially my family, would say if I didn't make it in my business. Life only happens once. If you have a burning desire to make a difference in this world, don't hesitate to take a leap of faith and make it happen.

ABOUT LEONOR GIL

Leonor Gil is a professional in the financial services industry with over thirty years of experience acquired as Senior Vice President at a top global institution, and as Director of Operations for Harris Associates L. P., a prominent Chicago advisory firm. Leonor is passionate about creating and implementing strategies to promote an inclusive and diverse work environment. Areas of expertise include process improvements and management and personnel management. Over the years, Leonor leveraged her strong business acumen by developing a panoramic view of the business working across various disciplines including Finance, Technology, HR, Compliance, and Client Servicing, to name a few.

Leonor is an advocate and strong supporter for diversity and inclusion and has served as the Treasurer, Secretary, and Co-Chair of the Professional Development Committee of the Latino Council. Leonor received the Chairman's Award – D&I in 2017 and the Mujeres de HACE Leadership Award in 2018. Leonor has been featured in various publications including *Profiles in Diversity Journal Magazine, Revista Agenda Mujer,* and the Daily Herald's Business Ledger, Influential Women in Business. Leonor enjoys sharing her knowledge by participating in different panels including finance, diversity in the workplace, and mentoring circles.

Leonor enjoys positively impacting the lives of others by volunteering for Big Brothers, Big Sister for United Way and as a Confirmation Facilitator at her church. She serves as a mentor to coworkers and to young Latinas for The

Fig Factor Foundation, where she has served as a board member, Secretary, and Treasurer. Leonor is a published contributing author in *Today's Inspired Latina Vol. V*; the soon-to-be-published *Business Divas: Stories of Women Leading in Business;* and *Today's Inspired Leader Vol. IV.* Leonor's motto is to "Live to Serve, and Serve to Live".

Leonor received a BA degree in Finance from the University of Houston, is fluent in Spanish, holds several FINRA licenses including Series 7, 24, 63, is a Life License producer, and has a Mentor Coach Certification.

Leonor is a proud mother or two children, Jorge and Carol, and a proud grandmother to four grandchildren: Destiny, Anthony, Santino, and Jaylani! Leonor loves to travel! Her hobbies include hiking, dancing, and spending quality time with the family.

Leonor Gil
LinkedIn: Leonor B. Gil
IG: @leogil12

A GIRL WITH A DREAM!

ELIZABETH BANERJEE

"Dream big, plan, act, and stay consistent because the possibilities are endless!"

I'm the first in my family with a graduate degree. After thirteen years of being out of school and much self-doubt, I decided to go back to school and pursue my master's in finance. Although it was difficult for me at the time, balancing my career, going to school, and being a mom and a wife, I was able to finish!

You see, I'm the first one in my family with a degree. My father only went to kindergarten. As one of the oldest, he had to leave school to work and help support the family after his father died. On the other hand, my mother was forced to leave school after sixth grade by her father because of the belief that "women get married, and their place is at home."

Knowing this, I made it my mission to get an education when I came to this country, an education my parents wished they had but could only dream of because they never had the opportunity to pursue it. I was going to make them proud!

I WAS EASILY REPLACEABLE!

It was only a few weeks after my graduate school registration, and I was about to receive the most important news that would cause a significant shift in my life. One day in January 2019, I received a call from my then-boss to tell me that my position as a manager for my banking center was being eliminated. Technology was taking over. I would no longer have my job starting June 2019 because they would have one manager manage two banking centers!

I know you may be thinking that at least they gave me ample time to look for something. Let me tell you, it was the worst feeling ever. My heart sank, and I remember crying like a baby in my office when I was given the news. I had worked so hard and overcame so many obstacles to finally manage my own banking center and build the perfect team! For what? I couldn't believe it was being taken away from me just like that!

After many sleepless nights, others crying myself to sleep, days of continuous job search, and many failed interviews, it dawned on me: I was easily replaceable! I went from feeling successful to being a failure. Although it had only been a few weeks of job searching within the company, it felt like an eternity. I was not getting a response, and my clock was ticking, so I decided to apply for positions outside the country—that is how desperate I had gotten.

I applied for positions in Paris, Argentina, Mexico City; you name it. The funny thing is, I actually got an interview in Paris. My family and I were traveling around that time to France, and I'm so glad I went because it changed my life. I showed up to the interview, and it was an experience.

How many people can say they had an interview in Paris? I remember the building was in one of the most expensive areas in France, right next to the Louis Vuitton store. There was a doorman guarding the entrance who almost didn't let me in. Once I explained I was there for an interview in my broken French, I went inside.

I was left speechless by the decor and royal-like ambiance. After being interviewed by one of the managers, I had a second interview with an executive director who looked at me and said something like, "You have an impressive resume, and you are overqualified for this position." Believe it or not, that's all I needed. I needed someone to acknowledge all my hard work and experience, which gave me the boost I needed. That made the whole trip worthwhile and was the cause of my shift in mindset.

I came back confident and sure of all I had to offer. I no longer applied for positions I was overqualified for but to ones I was not fully qualified for, knowing I may be able to obtain one. All this time, I doubted myself, and it showed that's why I was not getting hired. Having changed that, I could secure a position on my return. However, I had made a shift in priorities. All this time, I prioritized my job, career, and next promotion and put me and my family second. I knew my worth now; I had to continue to invest in myself and put my family first. This new job allowed me to do just that! I no longer had to work late hours or work weekends. This also allowed me to open my business.

I STARTED MY BUSINESS IN THE MIDDLE OF A PANDEMIC.

I was starting a new chapter in my life. I gained confidence, a new job, went back to school, and started my makeup business. I always dreamed of being my own boss but was never brave enough to pursue it. Year after year, I would let my ideas vanish with no action. I always filled my head with questions of "What will I do?" and "What if I fail?" instead of just going with my gut and just doing it!

It was my niece, who was sixteen at that time, who pushed me to open a business. She came to me one day and asked, "Tia, I want to open my own business. Can you help me?" I immediately said, "Yes, but I want in on it, and we will do this the right way!"

To this day, I don't think she knows that she helped me more than I helped her. She sparked something in me that day; she was that extra push that I needed, and I haven't looked back since. She had changed the question to, "What if we succeed?" We started Makeup Galore Inc. in July 2020 during a pandemic. For me, it was less scary having someone else take the journey with me.

At Makeup Galore, we have carefully curated makeup and cosmetics for Latina women and those who love the Latino culture. I don't know if you believe in speaking things into existence or the power of the mind, but I believe that's how Makeup Galore evolved! Believe it or not, I already had the domain name www.makeupgalore.com from years ago when I had contemplated opening a business.

I had no idea what my business would be, but I knew I loved makeup, loved the name, and had the opportunity to acquire it, thanks to my husband, who is part of the domain industry. I had even found the makeup wholesaler we used for our first order, six years before we opened the business!

I know it's hard to believe because I could not believe it when I saw the email I sent the wholesaler six years before establishing the business. I had wasted so much time doubting myself and waiting for the perfect time. Sometimes we overthink things and hold ourselves back. I always wanted to wait for everything to be perfect before I started. Now I know it will never be perfect, nor will it ever be an ideal time. We just have to work on perfecting the process. You have to act on it and work on it every day! So, no matter how small you think your idea or business may be, go for it anyway! Work toward your goal every day. What if you succeed?

I ALWAYS LOVED MAKEUP, BUT I DIDN'T THINK I WAS FIT TO BE IN THE BEAUTY INDUSTRY.

I've always loved makeup, but I didn't think I was fit to be in the beauty industry. I had never considered myself thin and beautiful like the girls in magazines. I did not go to a beauty school. To me, that was the image of beauty and fashion. This was one of the reasons why I hesitated for so long before opening my business. Even after opening my beauty business, I rarely posted any pictures of myself promoting my business. I always had my circle look at me and ask in disbelief, "You have a makeup business?"

So, yes, I was always worried about what they would

say and think. The truth is, it doesn't matter anymore. I soon realized it only matters how I feel, and I love makeup! I love seeing how it makes women feel when wearing it. I love the sudden boost in confidence it brings. It's like magic!

My love for makeup and entrepreneurship started at a young age. At four years old, I remember playing with my mother's makeup. She would give me the broken lipsticks and eyeshadows she no longer wanted. I remember I would put on her makeup, wear her heels, and be the happiest a four-year-old could be! Feeling grown and beautiful! I always looked at my mom as she put her makeup on; it was fascinating.

My mom has the most beautiful green eyes, and the eyeshadow made them pop out even more. I couldn't wait to be able to wear it one day. I still remember she gave me my first lipstick in seventh grade, and although it was a nude color and you could barely notice I had anything on, it made me feel beautiful.

Mom even allowed me to wear mascara, which later became a daily must-have. This was huge for me because not many girls could wear makeup at that age, making me feel more beautiful and confident. My love for makeup continued through the years. In college, I became a beauty consultant for MaryKay for extra income.

I loved helping other women feel beautiful, and I got products at a discount, so it was a win-win for me. I loved the women in my group, and I learned about the different products for different skin types and the different eyeshadow looks. Plus, I had a very supportive community in my group.

Being a beauty consultant increased my confidence

and ability to speak to anyone about beauty products. I don't remember how long I did it, but it lasted a few years after graduation. I still remember making beauty appointments even after I returned to Chicago after graduation.

Being a beauty consultant led me to another job in sales and marketing. This increased my sales experience as I went from business to business selling spa packages. Let me tell you, it was not an easy task! However, this job eventually led me into banking, where I have been for the last fifteen years.

Somewhere along the way, I lost myself. I became a mother, a wife, and a career woman. I was so consumed with different responsibilities and working for the next promotion that I forgot to take time for myself, and worst of all, I had forgotten my passion.

Thanks to the interview in Paris and my newfound confidence, I stepped outside my comfort zone and joined a mentorship group within my firm. I loved the connections I made and the mindset change that it brought me. I was ready for more. I decided to invest in myself and joined the Women's Institute of Self-Development and Efficacy.

This is important because although I already had my business established, I needed to invest in myself to become the CEO of Makeup Galore I needed to be. WISE took me to the next level. It increased my confidence and faith as I finally found a church I felt was for me and kept me accountable for the goals I had set for the program. It brought many new friendships, professional connections, and a very supportive community of women supporting women.

Once you start investing in yourself and see the value,

you can't stop! I found another mentorship group after WISE with IC U/Latina. For the first time, I felt someone knew the obstacles and barriers I had overcome as a Latina in finance, as a Latina woman entrepreneur, and they were there to uplift me and inspire me. Sometimes that is all we need: for someone to say, "I see you, girl!"

Once you awaken the passion lost inside you, you are unstoppable. So dream big. Although Makeup Galore is solely online and pop-ups occasionally, I continue to have big dreams for my company. Makeup Galore is bringing out the best in me; this is just the beginning! We are bringing confidence one woman at a time.

My Final Business Diva Word:

DREAM

You must give yourself permission to dream. Dreaming gives you access to all the possibilities. It is your vision and motivator for you to achieve bigger goals which would be impossible to reach otherwise.

ABOUT ELIZABETH BANERJEE

Elizabeth Banerjee is a proud native of Guanajuato, Mexico, and currently resides in Chicago, Illinois. She is the President and CEO of Makeup Galore Inc., a company that sells quality makeup products and promotes self-care specially curated for Latinas and those who love the Latino culture. Elizabeth is on a mission to help increase women's confidence through makeup and to inspire other women entrepreneurs.

When Elizabeth is not running her business or writing a book, she is working in the banking industry, where she has held various professional positions for the last fifteen years. She holds degrees in international business from Bethune-Cookman University, and a master's in finance from the University of Arizona. She is a member of Sigma Alpha Iota, the Women's Institute of Self-Development & Efficacy, and recently participated in IC U/Latinas cohort 3. Elizabeth is heavily committed to community service and leading volunteer efforts. She believes in giving back and supporting our underserved communities.

Elizabeth Banerjee
elizabethbanerjee20@gmail.com
IG: @makeupgaloreonline
FB: Makeup Galore
Tik Tok: @makeupgaloreinc
www.makeupgalore.com

JEANETTE ARTEAGA

The wings of transformation are born of patience and struggle. — *Janet S. Dickens*

I've been an entrepreneur for as far back as I can remember. In Pilsen, 17th and Laflin is where it all began. I was selling *agua de horchata* and lemonade with my cousin Anabel in front of our apartment building. My mom gave us the recipe and my dad helped carry the big jugs downstairs. We had quite a few customers; even the *gangeros* would stop and support our little business. I soon upgraded to selling gold— well, my sister's gold rings. Can you believe she still won't let me forget about that? My mother says *que me parezco a mi abuela,* Mama China. She was a fierce woman and an entrepreneur. My Tía Salud and her would make and sell candy to the surrounding ranchos, so I guess you can say entrepreneurship runs in my blood.

Growing up, both my parents worked at Nabisco—yes,

they made Oreo and Chip Ahoy cookies. They would try to work opposite shifts so someone was always home, but sometimes my sister Lilia got stuck with us. She would take me to her cheerleading practice at Juarez HS or swimming at Harrison Park. I was nine years old when my parents purchased our home and moved us from Pilsen to Chicago Lawn so they could be closer to their job. My sister soon got married and we were left with *"No le abran la puerta a nadie."* Now that I'm grown, I don't know how my parents managed with six children, because we were a handful.

LIFE BEGINS

Becoming a mother at sixteen was not in my plans. I felt like I had let my family down. "I should've whooped you," my sister said jokingly as she hugged my baby, "but then we wouldn't have this little angel." My baby was such a blessing, and he brightened up the house with so much joy. I stepped away from school for a year to be with my son and later returned as a junior. By senior year I became a single mother, but my family stepped up to help me with Jorgie so that I could continue with my education.

One day after school, I decided to go to the Avon office on 59th & Kedzie. I was looking for a purse that my best friend Julia purchased and I just had to have one. "Have you ever thought about selling Avon?" the director asked. "You'd be really good at it." I thought to myself, *Why not? Everyone buys Avon anyway.* I was only seventeen when I began attending meetings, handing out Avon books in my neighborhood, and hanging around ladies much older than me.

Side note: For those thinking about joining a direct selling business or are in one already, try it out for a while! Whether you stay with it or not, you will gain skills, confidence, and life experiences that are invaluable in anything you decide to pursue. This was my introduction to networking, marketing, and self-development.

Once I graduated high school, I stopped selling Avon. I was entering a new chapter in my life. I started college at St. Xavier, but as a single mother, I needed to get a "real job." I began to work at TCF Bank in Oak Lawn, and within the first month, I realized I was good at sales. I was so excited because I exceeded my sales goal and hit my bonus, but then my manager decided I didn't qualify. I cried. She took what I earned away because she underestimated me. I was so upset, but I made sure I hit my goal every month, I worked hard, and within a few months, I became a supervisor. Ms. Robynn Fortner, another influential woman in my life, was a manager from a different branch. She saw my potential and took me with her when she left the bank. I was now twenty-three years old making more than I ever did until I got in my own way.

THE STRUGGLES

In my mid-twenties I had lost my job and my apartment. I was a hot mess and saw myself as a failure and a burden to my family. My self-esteem was all the way to the floor. How was I going to be a good mother? I truly believed everyone was better off without me. I fell into a deep depression, wasting days away in my room, in and out of sleep and not knowing what time of day it was. My mom would come into my room clap her hands and say, "Action, Jeanette, action, *párate y lucha, que nada es imposible.*"

I ended up ditching all my meds, but it was time to see my doctor again. Thankfully, she was on maternity leave, because my new doctor was able to diagnose me with ADHD. It was easy for her to recognize it because she had it herself. For years I struggled with poor time management, being easily distracted, and impulsiveness. Eventually, anxiety and depression were added to the mix. I was so relieved once I knew what it was because I could not figure out what was wrong with me. I can't imagine how my mom felt seeing her baby in a dark place.

I finally left the house because my mom wanted to go to my cousin Erica's Jewelry party. I definitely needed time with my family, and at the end of the party, I felt the direct-selling business was calling my name once again. I decided to become a Lia Sophia advisor, and it was one of the best choices I made. I loved working alongside these beautiful ladies because Anne Soto, our team director, had created a sisterhood environment. This was the first time I ever felt genuine support and empowerment with a group of ladies and without competition because we wanted each other to win.

By the time my son was in high school, I decided to give college another try. I went back for business management at my community college, Richard J. Daley. I made myself property manager for my family's rental properties and helped my brothers with their construction company. In 2011, my son's father came back into my life after being "away" for seven years. He began to work with my brothers, and shortly after, we rekindled our relationship and decided it was best to give our family another try. Our precious little gemstone, Ruby, came into our lives in 2013. After sixteen years, my son got his wish of being a brother and having his dad back home. Everything seemed good, everyone was healthy, we were all together, and thank God *nada me faltaba*.

A few years later, my father began to show symptoms of multiple sclerosis. At this crucial time, my parent's health insurance was switched and my parents didn't know the details of what they had signed for. This opened up a conversation about life insurance. I was so nervous to ask my dad if he had any life insurance. I imagined him saying *"Ya quieres que me muera?"* but I finally asked and he directed me to his pension department. To our surprise, they said once he retired, so did his life insurance. Okay, not a big deal, we'd just have to get some, so I began shopping around.

THE TRANSFORMATION

Unfortunately, the older you get, the more it costs, and you still have to get approved. The original quote we received was out of our budget because my parents were retired and now had health issues. Thankfully, a few weeks later I was invited to a presentation on retirement, life insurance, and a few other things. The information I learned was so valuable that I wished I had known about it sooner. Something inside me woke up and I thought to myself, *This is it!* This was the inspiration I needed and the path I was going to take to create my career. I was so eager to learn all about insurance that I got licensed within a week. Amazingly, six years later, I hold four licenses in two states and opened up my own insurance agency, Monarca Insurance & Financial Partners, in Chicago Lawn near Midway.

It was very important that I open my office in my neighborhood. The vision I had was to serve and help the people I saw every day like my neighbors and the surrounding businesses I frequented. I am one of over thirty insurance companies within a few miles, so I had to set myself apart from everyone else. I needed to share who I was, what I liked to do, and what I felt was important. I began to host pop-ups to create a platform for small businesses. I offered small business vendors a space to hold workshops for kids, and I began to host financial classes and other community events.

Starting a business has been tremendously hard work. On any given day, you will see my lights on at eleven p.m.; you would think I was getting paid overtime, but no, it's just the price we pay as entrepreneurs. Don't get me wrong, I love what I do, but it's easy to get stressed! Balancing my business, making time for family, and taking time for self-care is challenging. Although my mom has made a tempting offer. She tells me to stop working and just stay home with her. When I finally agree, she changes her tune and says, *"No, no más sal temprano."* Thankfully, my parents have always been supportive, because giving up is not an option.

We will all face many challenges throughout our lifetime. In our personal lives and in business. You will fall and you will encounter doubters *y gente envidiosa*, but the biggest challenge, the biggest struggle, will be your own self-doubt. I self-sabotaged countless opportunities because I didn't think

I was good enough—I didn't have a college degree, I was a single mother, I literally came up with every excuse in the book on why I couldn't do something. The truth was I was afraid of letting myself down again. It has taken me years of healing to say "it's OK, these things happen."

ALAS PARA VOLAR

I've learned to forgive and accept myself because there is nothing wrong with me. I've embraced my ADHD because its allows me to work from a different perspective. It is my gift, it is my superpower. I didn't need to live up to anyone's expectations but my own. My journey is mine, no matter how long it takes. All the roadblocks, failures, and mistakes are part of my growth. We will always have doubts and challenges in different aspects and stages of our lives, but trust that the struggle will give you strength, courage, and wisdom para volar! Always surround yourself with *mujeres chingonas porque ellas te van a dar ánimo* when you feel yourself slipping. My main support is my sister; she is always there to lift me up. I am doing things I never even imagined myself capable of doing because she pushed me on days I didn't believe in myself.

I chose the name *Monarca* for my business because they are a symbol of beauty, strength, and transformation. It is crucial for a butterfly to struggle because it's the struggle that gives her wings the strength to fly. Every year I travel back to my roots in Michoacan, Mexico, just like the *Monarca,* to recharge and humble myself so I don't lose sight of what's important in my life. I love and embrace my rich culture, and through my business, I want to help my people. I take educating people in my community very seriously so they can make informed financial decisions. I also try to run a business with integrity, respect, and kindness as my top priority.

I am grateful for all the small businesses that help make our events successful, our partnerships, and the customers that have supported and trusted us along the way. I am grateful for my family and for all the love and support they have given me throughout my life. A special thank you to Elizabeth Banerjee & Martha Razo, who encouraged me to write my story. Most importantly, I am grateful to God for blessing me and guiding me to this day.

"Action, párate y lucha, que nada es imposible."
—Carmen Arteaga

My Final Business Diva Word:

VOLAR

Your wings already exist, *nomás tienes que volar!*

ABOUT JEANETTE ARTEAGA

Jeanette Arteaga is a first-generation Latina born and raised in Chicago. She is a Farmers Agency owner and founder of Monarca Insurance & Financial Partners, Inc., where she provides insurance, credit repair, and income tax services.

Her mission is to empower her community through education so they can make informed decisions in creating their financial foundation. Her office also offers small business owners support, hosts various community events for kids, and educational workshops for parents.

She is a board member of the Southwest Chamber of Commerce, a member of W.I.S.E. Women's Institute of Self-Development of Efficacy, and a graduate of the W.I.S.E. Leadership & Coaching Program and of ICU/Latinas Cohort 3.

Jeanette is a mother of two and the new glam mother of an adorable baby boy. She loves to travel, but her favorite place is going back to Michoacan, Mexico, with her parents to their family home.

Jeanette Arteaga
Phone: 773-701-5000
Monarca Insurance & Financial Partners
monarca.financial@gmail.com
www.monarcafinancial.com

A SOARING EAGLE

ROSARIO SANCHEZ

"I can truly say that I am living my ancestors' wildest dreams! And I don't even need to go that far back. I am living my parents' wildest dreams."

"*¡Usted es chingona, mija!*" These were my father's words growing up. They rang in my ear as if he was still here. Whenever I faced adversity, he would remind me that I was in charge of my life and my future and that it was up to me to make things happen.

One of the many things that I am very grateful for is my parents' love and support. I tell everyone how I never had luxury growing up, but I had the most valuable and expensive asset at home: LOVE. Also, some very strict parents only wanted what was best for me. I can never thank them enough for everything they did to ensure I walked on the right path.

As a girl who grew up in El Barrio, I never thought I would be in the business I am in now. I have been doing real estate for the past five years and I love it!

I started working in the customer service field at the age of seventeen. Working as a teller at a currency exchange at a young age allowed me to leverage my knowledge, and I decided to try retail banking. I was in retail banking for six years and decided it was time to change.

I loved working with people and helping them with their financial needs. I came across the opportunity to do real estate, and even though, at first, I couldn't see how rewarding it would be, real estate has now become my passion. Now I am a successful mompreneur selling Chicago and surrounding areas!

MY STORY BEGINS IN MEXICO

At the age of five, my mother decided that it was best that we move to the US with my father and his family. My brother was only a few months old, and the economy in Mexico was not looking that promising. Looking for a better future for my brother and me, she left her family behind and, with all the pain in her heart, didn't look back.

I still remember the fear and excitement of arriving at a brand-new place. Everything looked crowded and much taller than I was used to in our town back in Mexico. We had not seen my dad in months, and the one thing I won't forget about that night when we arrived was him carrying me up the stairs into the home where we would be staying.

Like many families that come to this country, we lived with other family members. It wasn't long until we had our own apartment and a bedroom I could call my own.

Coming to a new country where we needed to adjust to

a different language and culture was difficult. I was made fun of because I didn't understand or know the language of those closest to me and in school. I remember sitting down in the school cafeteria, trying to figure out what the other students were saying, and it makes me smile to this day.

Even though it was a bit frustrating in the beginning being the bright little girl that I had always been, I quickly picked up the English language. It's as if, by instinct, I knew I had no choice but to adjust. From first to third grade, I was in bilingual classes, and by the time I was in fourth grade, the school decided it was time for me to be in an all-English classroom.

I excelled in all my classes throughout elementary and high school. Not only because I loved school but also because my dad would have killed me if I came home with bad grades. I always enjoyed setting goals for getting straight As, and graduating with honors from high school was one of them.

While in school, I found myself fascinated with AutoCAD and decided I wanted to attend architecture school. Unfortunately, the dreams of attending school and becoming an architect quickly crumbled. My parents had recently separated, and the dream of attending college was out the door. I cried as I saw my friends going away for school, and it took me a few months to get over the fact that I couldn't do the same.

I could see my mom struggling to make ends meet, and the best thing for me to do was to get a job as soon as I graduated to help her with her expenses. I do not know how my mom managed to care for my brother and me while I was still in school. I will forever admire her strength and determination.

While working full-time as a teller at the currency, I decided that I could go to school part-time, but that was challenging. It would take me years to receive any degree, but I kept pushing through, taking a few classes here and there.

The year 2010 was a defining year in my life. This year was filled with many blessings and the unexpected news that I would be laid off. When this happened, I was three months pregnant with my Kamilah. I did everything to stay positive but quickly noticed that the workforce was not too friendly with pregnant women. Not only was finding a job a struggle during that time, but also the relationship I was in. I remember crying in the middle of my kitchen and asking myself how I got to this place. I felt blessed and grateful for my baby, but that was not the type of life I aspired to be growing up.

You see, I had created this roadmap, a plan for my life. I was going to graduate high school, attend college, and become an architect. Get a good job and buy my mom her dream home. But as I stood there crying my eyes out, I realized that was my plan, not God's.

WHAT I DIDN'T KNOW AT THE TIME

That moment was defining in my life. As I cried and asked why, something spoke to me. I realized I would not be pregnant forever and would do everything to give her a better future once the baby was born. I had found a strong WHY in my life; if I had always pushed to accomplish my goals now, I needed to push even harder.

I applied to several banking positions when my daughter was only a few months old. In November 2011, I began working as a twenty-hour teller. That was the beginning of God's plan for my daughter and me.

Retail banking was a much more professional environment. I saw the opportunities that it offered, so I gave it my all. I had goals, and I knew I would accomplish them. Just like a diamond in the rough, I was polished and shining brighter than ever. I learned as much as possible, and within a few years, I was promoted. It wasn't long before I made enough money to rent my own place. This allowed me to leave the toxic environment I had been in, and life was inviting me into a new season.

Knowledge is power! I used all the skills I had gained from working all those years in the customer service field and brought them into real estate. Like I mentioned before, never in my wildest dreams did I ever think I would be helping others achieve their American Dream.

My parents rented their whole life, and I never knew the importance of home ownership. Coming into the field, I quickly noticed a lack of knowledge in our communities and felt that it was my duty to do something about it. I think back to when I was growing up; I wonder what would've happened if there had been someone there to show, educate, and inform my family and me about home ownership. Things like credit and other lending requirements should be taught in our schools or anywhere in our communities more.

My passion comes from my family's struggles; I am that person that I would have loved to have grown up; I strive to be that person that educates, informs, and holds people's hand through the home-buying process.

Not only was getting my real estate a huge blessing and a life-changing moment, but buying my own home was a beautiful accomplishment for my family and me. Living in Pilsen, we never knew what it was like to have a backyard. Our cookouts were on the sidewalk, so we didn't even know a thing about having our own grass. When I bought my home, my life changed!

We found so much value in the small things because we knew how hard our journey had been. I enjoyed seeing my mom watering the grass or finally having a cookout in our own backyard. That year my mother was diagnosed with stage four cancer, and was only with us for eight months after that. Losing my parents was not easy, but I know it sure made me strong. It pushed me to get out of my comfort zone and want to fly into higher places.

My mom would always bring up stories about eagles. She would mention how eagles are different from any other bird species; eagles flew higher and, for the most part, flew alone. *Las águilas vuelan solas!* That was her saying, and it didn't really hit until I found myself in a place where I needed to be strong and fly solo.

Yes, I surrounded myself with great people that inspired me, but I had to leave the fear behind and do things on my own. My daughter has been my biggest priority, and showing her that there will be times we need to roll up our sleeves and do things on our own is a big lesson I have been teaching her.

I always questioned the whys in my life, but now I know to be grateful for the good and the bad. My business has been growing and continues to grow. Life will always give lessons;

I know that I wouldn't have the drive and determination to do anything if I had not gone through those lessons.

Real estate has changed my life and has allowed me to help and change so many other people's lives. It is now my passion to inform and educate the community. Many people come into the field because they hear how much money they can make. Yes, the money can be good, but the best thing about working in real estate is that amazing feeling you get at the end knowing that you helped another family.

Many people come to me thinking they can never be a homeowner. This always takes me back to my family and I living in a small two-bedroom apartment in Pilsen. We never thought we could own a home, and at times it wouldn't even cross our minds.

There's so much misinformation that goes around about real estate and the process of owning it, that many people become discouraged and never pursue that dream. I must inform and educate the community about real estate and guide them toward achieving their goal.

Being honest and genuine in this field is also very important. People will sense whether you're coming from a place of ambition or if you care about their family and investment. It all comes down to trust; that's why it is so important for your WHY to be more than just monetary.

My Final Business Diva Word:

TENACIOUS

Today I find myself thankful not only for all the good God has done in my life, but I am also thankful for the dark moments. Those moments when we are tested are the most defining in our life. Diamonds, butterflies, and pearls are known to grow in darkness and under pressure. Those beautiful creations are a reminder when faced with adversity to keep moving forward. I will continue to share my testimony and continue to inspire and encourage others to pursue their dreams.

ABOUT ROSARIO SANCHEZ

Rosario Sanchez has been in the real estate industry for the past five years. She is a dedicated mom, investor, and entrepreneur. Despite the many adversities in her life, she has built a successful career. As a mompreneur, she is passionate about empowering women and encourages them to find their why.

Her story begins in Mexico, and at a young age moved to the city of Chicago. She lived most of her life in Pilsen with her parents and younger brother. After witnessing the many struggles her family faced by the lack of knowledge in financial literacy, she believes in the importance of educating and informing the community on this subject. Her biggest motivation in life is living with purpose and her daughter Kamilah.

Rosario Sanchez
rosario@goldenhomes.com
Phone: 312-420-1484
Facebook: facebook.com/rosario.sanchez.566

I SAID YES

BLANCA SEPULVEDA

"When you know yourself, you are empowered. When you accept yourself, you are invincible." —Tina Lifford

FAMILY FOUNDATION

I dedicate my story to my dear grandmother Rosa. She passed away as I approved the final edits. My grandmother gave me a loving foundation and a great example of hard work and resilience. My grandmother was my first hero. I was mesmerized by learning her story of moving from her birthplace, Autlán, Jalisco, MX, to the US per her mom's, my great-grandmother's, advice to work in the States and purchase a home for herself. She worked many jobs, including waitressing and housekeeping, and she saved every penny. She had to be disciplined for many years, forsaking instant gratification; she had to tell her children "no" to their simple wants to save for their needs. She married my grandfather, a police officer, but he passed away when my mom and uncle

117

were very young. As a single mom, she was disciplined and determined, and she worked hard to purchase her home. She sacrificed, leaving her children behind twice, to make this dream possible. I also admire how responsible and organized she was.

While away, her children grew up and started their own families in their early twenties before she could finally make it happen with them. She had a home built in Ensenada, and her son could build upon it with his new family until he was ready for his own home. She was always so generous. She also bought a house in the northern suburbs of Chicago. She always lived alone. I remember my sisters and me visiting her on the weekends with my mom. She was still working with no days off. We would arrive while she was still on her shift at work, and we would not see her until first thing in the morning, with breakfast ready. She was always cheerful and giving. I'll never forget the delicious Christmas cookies she baked every year.

When she retired, she sold both her homes and moved into her new custom-built home in her hometown of Autlán. She let me know that God had multiplied her blessings because she was generous to all those in need, considering the little she had. My grandmother enjoyed her retirement, and we visited each other often; she always traveled alone. During her last years in retirement, when she couldn't travel any longer, she kept sharp by playing her favorite board game, Rummikub, daily. My grandmother had an excellent memory and sound mind until her last breath. She was very competitive and won most of the games we played against her. She hated to lose, and I loved that competitiveness in her. She also knitted and loved spending time with family. She had such a great sense of humor, making everyone laugh.

In 2016, she was diagnosed with stage 4 cancer, and for six years, she battled it and never complained of her illness. We were blessed to have the extra time to be with her. On her last birthday, at ninety-one, she celebrated with family, enjoyed her favorite mariachi music, and could dance to a couple of songs, even for a few seconds. Unfortunately, the next day she peacefully passed away. I was and still am heartbroken. I lost a spark of light in my soul when she left us. I knew the day would come, but I didn't think it would be this soon. She was ready to go, and I had to accept it was her time. I miss her so much. We were very close, and I loved my grandmother with all my heart and soul. I miss her every day.

My father worked as a plant manager at Zenith Electronics for twenty years and as a car mechanic on the weekends. He showed me hard work and was a great example of giving back and helping others in need.

My parents divorced when I was seventeen. Financial struggles were the primary reason for their separation.

I had my first glimpse of entrepreneurship from my mom. As a stay-at-home mom, she helped bring in extra income as a beautician, by babysitting, carpooling, baking cakes, and making piñatas. Growing up, I admired her. She was strong and very generous and caring. When my parents divorced, my mom started to work in a factory. Eventually, she worked in housekeeping in a hospital and 911 center until she retired to go and care for my grandmother in Mexico eight years ago.

My first job was as a bank teller, then a customer service representative, and at the age of twenty-two, I started working at the Federal Reserve Bank of Chicago, where I worked for twenty years. Around the same time, I was dating my high school sweetheart, and we had our son at the age of twenty-three. I realized that we had different goals in life and decided to end the relationship and raise my son alone.

COMMUNITY ACTIONS

During high school, I got involved with my local community. My first meeting was with an organization called LOBO, Latinos of Berwyn and Cicero. I remember being young and learning about issues in our community and the importance of helping fellow Latinos.

When I turned eighteen, I became a voter registrant. I would sit outside storefronts and walk around festivals, urging people to register to vote to ensure they had a voice. I also got involved in immigration rights and went to Washington, DC, to attend my first protest. I didn't see myself pursuing a career in politics, but it was essential to be responsible, make a difference, and create a more powerful voice together. These efforts began my love to take action in empowering others.

I was involved in community outreach at the bank and volunteered with various not-for-profit organizations. I was part of initiating the bank's employee support network group, the Latino Resource Association (LRA), and was on the board for four years. I volunteered for the United States Hispanic Leadership Institute's (USHLI) annual conference for many years and enjoyed helping high school students transition into college.

In addition, I volunteered with Junior Achievement (JA), a nonprofit that goes into the schools and teaches students about money. Through JA, students learn about needs and wants, our communities, money, banking, economics, budgeting, starting a business, résumé building, and interviewing. I found the program fascinating and incredibly important. I even taught my son when I got home, since he didn't have this program available at his school. JA will always be near and dear to my heart. My heart is in philanthropy, where I not only give my time but also give back financially. Financial freedom allows us to do more, help more, and is much more rewarding. I learned that we need to be ready to act as God nudges and inspires us to help meet the needs of others.

INVESTMENT IN KNOWLEDGE

In 2012, I attended a personal finance workshop. I heard about money concepts I needed help understanding, like the power of compound interest, fewer taxes, and assessing financial health. It reminded me of JA but applied to the period after high school when people started earning money and making crucial decisions. Organizations like JA exist because no classes in school teach us about money. So why don't these classes exist in our schools?

With the newfound concepts, I realized that my grandmother, who had worked hard, saved, and sacrificed all her life, could have had much more, faster. My family could have spent more time together instead of always working multiple jobs, and my parents would have fought less about money. I was disturbed as well as intrigued. I worked a part-time job to make extra income and saw my grandmother and parents' lives unfolding within me. *How is that possible?* I asked myself, repeating the same generational patterns.

I wanted to learn more and share this essential information with my son, who had just turned sixteen and started his first job—how I wished I had been educated with financial knowledge when I was his age! But, unfortunately, we don't know what we don't know.

Today, I am so proud of him. Not only does my son have a good heart, but he's also responsible. He's a hard worker and implements critical financial strategies for a better future. How powerful it is to make a difference for the next generation! I am grateful that he will have a different, positive experience to pass on to his children someday.

Working in banking had helped, but it wasn't enough. I remember being in debt as early as my twenties. I've always worked two jobs. I was waitressing and bartending part-time because I wanted to buy a house, put my son in private school, and travel. I would need more than my bank job to realize my goals and dreams.

I like to work, but I started questioning my position at the bank and found it could have been more rewarding. I wanted to help people, be my own boss, and double my income, but that seemed far-fetched. Where would I find such an ideal position? I thought I would need a significant investment to become a business owner, and I found it wasn't true. However, with the right platform and mentorship, I could start part-time, so I would not have to quit the bank immediately. So I said yes, got out of my comfort zone, and started my new career.

Financial services is a lucrative industry. I was amazed! I started making more money part-time than I was making full-time at the bank. It was amazing for me to witness the power of entrepreneurship firsthand!

I saw a demand to serve the community, sit down with families free of charge, educate them, assess their needs, and go over their goals regardless of their income or savings. It was a win-win situation!

Everyone deserves the same courtesy, whether you want to invest $50 a month or six figures. Financial security is within reach for everyone. It doesn't matter if you just started your first job or are about to retire. So many people need help and guidance. Do you know your FIN? Your financial independence number? I was so excited that I would be helping families in a multimillion-dollar industry.

After learning and becoming skilled at following a simple system, I took a leap of faith, left my career at the Federal Reserve Bank, and haven't looked back.

As the population ages and life expectancies rise, demand for financial planning services should increase too. I plan to be there, helping those who need help the most.

YOU ARE A PRODUCT OF YOUR ENVIRONMENT

As business owners, we will always have ups and downs. But, with faith and resilience, we will conquer fear and overcome adversity. I've learned that as long as we focus on personal development, we will gain the confidence we need to grow. God is my coach. I work for Him. I am stronger, braver, and more grateful for the people God has placed in my life. We must be true to ourselves. Meet him halfway by taking action, and everything will fall into place. He will open doors, but first, we must get uncomfortable by taking the first steps.

My goal is to bring others into finance through internships and mentoring programs. There are also comparatively few women role models and mentors in finance. I'm building a big team; my team is my extended family. I want to help them reach their goals as we help families. We are on a mission to help two million families nationwide by 2030. Everyone is worthy of success, but we have to surround ourselves with individuals who are doing what we strive to do and be. Our environment is essential. I have met some great people who have helped me along my journey, and I want to do the same for others. I thank God for my mentors and friends and look forward to building many more relationships and friendships. Our purpose is to serve and to pay it forward. My next chapter is partnering with a non for profit that helps children who lost their parents. What better way to serve than to help those who can't help themselves? Please get in touch with me if you'd like to be part of this mission to make a difference for children: Niños Desamparados Todos Por Uno En México.

"When a flower doesn't bloom, you fix the environment in which it grows, not the flower."
—Alexander Den Heijer

My Final Business Diva Word:

FAITH

ABOUT BLANCA SEPULVEDA

Blanca, driven by economic transformation, uplifts individuals and communities toward generational prosperity. Blanca's background is in banking, and she spent twenty years at the Federal Reserve Bank of Chicago (FRBC). However, Blanca took a bold leap of faith and followed her passion; she quit her corporate job at the FRBC to open up her own business, Transformation Financial. She is an award-winning, nationally licensed financial expert who mentors, trains, and develops other individuals to become entrepreneurs.

Her company helps families from all walks of life create an independent financial future. She is passionate about giving back to the community and partners with many community-based organizations and businesses to bring financial awareness and implement financial strategies and solutions for families and individuals through workshops and complimentary consultations. Over the years, she has continued to advocate and support community social causes for the betterment of society and legacy building with solutions at the forefront. Blanca is a woman of faith. She proudly serves as a NAHREP 10 Certified Trainer.

Blanca serves on the Board of the Fig Factor Foundation, is a contributing author in *Today's Inspired Latina (Vol 5)*, and is an inspiration agent for Young Latina Day (April 11th). She has been a committee member/volunteer of Junior Achievement of Chicago, Rotary Little Village-Chicago, Prospanica/SEP, and Women of ALPFA. Blanca was also recognized in Who's Who, Negocios Now, Chicago's Suburbs (July 2021) and The Daily

Gerald's Business Ledger, Influential Women in Business (Oct 2020). Blanca is a certified JMT member of the John Maxwell Team. She loves traveling and spending time with family and is a proud mom of her son, Christian.

Blanca Sepulveda
blanca@transformation.financial
Phone: 708-426-9024

From Stay-at-Home Mom to Business Owner

LAURA ALCANTAR LEON

"He who perseveres, achieves"
"El que persevera, alcanza"

My name is Laura. I was born in 1987 in Las Trojes, Municipio de Alvaro Obregon, Michoacan, Mexico, and raised in Grand Rapids, Michigan, USA. I come from a small family of four: my father, Marcelino; my mother, Leticia; and my brother, Arturo. Ever since I was a little girl, I always wanted to become an architect. I had good grades and loved school. Until I met my husband, Salvador. I met my husband Salvador during my senior year in high school. I remember I was so excited about my senior pictures and everything regarding prom. I met him one day in January. The story of how we met is another story.

But from the first time we met, I felt something I had never felt before: love.

We dated for a year and a half. And on June 2008, we said "I do." So, needless to say, I did not finish high school. I lost my focus and got behind in my classes, which devastated me, but I never regretted marrying the love of my life. But it hurt not being able to accomplish the goal of graduating that I had always dreamed of. Years passed and I fell pregnant with our first child, our daughter Yamilet. I was the happiest woman alive. I always wanted to be a mother. With that amazing joy also came back bad memories of my past. When I was four years old, a family member molested me. I hid that for all my life from everyone out of fear when I was little, and as I grew up, I hid it out of shame and disgust until I met my husband. I opened up to him about what had happened to me in my childhood. I was scared, not knowing how he would react. But he assured me it wasn't my fault, that I was just a baby, and that it did not change the love he had for me.

But when my daughter was born, it triggered my PTSD. I told my husband that I did not want anyone to babysit our daughter, and that I wanted to personally care for her. And I thank God every day for being able to be a stay-at-home mom, and being able to care for my children personally. So, years passed, and four years later, our second child was born. We both agreed that once our baby went to kindergarten, I would go back to school or work.

The time came, and our second and youngest son, Isidro, started school. I wanted to finish my high school diploma to see if that would help me find a better-paying job. So I did. I requested my high school transcripts to learn I was only 1.5 credits short of graduating. That depressed me, knowing I could have potentially still been able to graduate on time, but I didn't because I got so upset when my counselor told me that I was short on credits, and I probably wouldn't be able to graduate.

So, after crying for a couple of minutes, I went to get started on completing my high school diploma. I finished the classes that I needed in a week and was able to finish my high school diploma in May 2020.

After that, I started looking for a job, thinking that with that diploma, I was suddenly going to be able to find a good-paying job. I was so wrong. Since I had not worked in over ten years, I had no relevant experience in anything. I had several failed interviews. I felt so frustrated. I felt like a loser. I was the only one without a degree in my immediate family. My husband had worked so hard all these years to provide for me and our children that I really wanted to start helping him with these big responsibilities.

That is when I started to think about my husband's dream, a dream he had always talked to me about for years: to start a pallet company. My husband has been working in the pallet industry for many years. Even though it is a very physical job, he enjoys it. He had talked to me several times about starting a pallet business, which I always shut down for fear of failure. I had been scared to invest our savings in something that had the chance of not succeeding—that is, until it felt like the only way to get a job. I finally started therapy to help me overcome the trauma I had dragged on all these years since I was a little girl. I knew that if I wanted to be able to succeed in the workforce, I needed help. And it really did help.

I built up the courage and formed my company in December 2020. In the spring of 2021, I started to look for a warehouse. In June of 2021, I had the keys to our warehouse. We started without any loans from banks or family. We started very small. We started with our savings. I did not want any debt.

At first, it was very hard. My husband has many years of experience working in the pallet industry, from repairing and building to dismantling pallets. He had no clue about what happens inside the office, though. I felt so lost; I had taken the job of managing a business all on my own, with no experience, knowledge, or training.

I went from a stay-at-home mom to being responsible for sales, bookkeeping, account receivables, account payables, shipping, and receiving, all on my own. I was so overwhelmed. But I felt confident in myself. My husband always told me I had everything in me to do that and more. I believed him. And I knew that I couldn't let him down. He had so much faith in me that it made me believe I really could do it all.

The first few months, I barely slept. I was always studying the industry, learning as much as possible, from where the lumber and scrap pallets are obtained to the most needed pallet sizes to how a pallet is built. I knew that if I was going to own and manage a pallet company, I needed to know as much as possible about the industry. I spent so many sleepless nights, so many hours in front of my computer, and made many calls and emails. I had pallets on my mind 24/7.

Four months later, we were blessed to start our business. I remember the day we shipped our first load, we were over the moon. We were so excited. That motivated me even more to keep going. I felt so proud of myself like never before. The feeling of loading that first shipment felt so encouraging. This industry is a rollercoaster. At least that is how it felt for me the first year, as I was getting to know and learn how this business works.

The year 2022 has been a year of learning, stress, sweat, tears, and growth. We have outgrown our warehouse and had to rent additional storage space. I have met amazing people in this industry and not-so-great ones as well. I now can hire a dedicated CPA to advise me year-round on the accounting aspect of my business. I still do my own bookkeeping, sales, account receivables, and payables. It is hard work, and that is never going to change. But as the business grows, it will make it easier to hire professionals and experienced people to help me manage my business. My goal is to eventually have my business generating income without requiring my daily presence.

From experience, I can tell you there isn't anything you can't do. No matter what society, family, friends, or anyone says. Having an academic education is important. It makes everything easier—a lot easier. But not having a degree is not a death sentence to your dream. Society tends to make it seem that the only way to success is obtaining a degree. Since kindergarten, we are taught to finish school, go to college, and prepare ourselves to be the best qualifying employee we can be. And that is a good path, but is not the only path.

Do not feel discouraged if you do not have a degree. Life happens, and sometimes, even if you wanted it, it doesn't happen. That does not mean you are a loser or that you are destined to fail. It only means you will have to work twice as hard to make it happen. I started my business without a degree, experience, or knowledge of the industry, without loans from banks, family, or friends. The one thing I did have was an abundance of dedication and hard work. Being my own boss is a lot of stress and hard work, but also it is the best decision I could have made.

My advice to you is to work hard, learn to manage your money, and save, save, save as much as possible. If your business qualifies for grants, apply for them. Invest wisely and do not take out big loans with banks; use your own funds or talk to investors. Start as little as you can afford, that way you will start profiting sooner than if you had debt. And above all, stay resilient and you will succeed!

My Final Business Diva Word:

RESILIENT

ABOUT LAURA ALCANTAR

Laura Alcantar Leon was born in Michoacan, Mexico, and raised in Grand Rapids, Michigan. She is the founder and owner of S & L PALLETS LLC, a pallet company in Wyoming, Michigan.

Before becoming a businesswoman, Laura was a stay-at-home mom who devoted her time raising her two children and making sure that her family was well taken care of. After nine years of dedicating herself to her family, she decided to support her husband's dream of starting a pallet company. With only one and a half years in business, Laura has managed to grow her business at an unexpected rate and continues to do so. She is proof that no matter how many obstacles life puts you through, if you persevere, you can achieve anything!

Laura Alcantar Leon
sandlpallets@gmail.com

VERONICA LUNA

"Échale ganas, no te rindas."

My name is Veronica. I come from a humble family that, with a lot of work, determination and sacrifice, my parents carried on and moved forward in life. I am from a town called Santa Catarina Morelos. I studied there only until ninth grade. My father was a farmer. He taught us what it means to work in the field planting corn, tomatoes, squash, and beans. I went to the market to sell when I was between six and seven years old. I sold *casahuate* mushrooms, depending on the season. I also sold *chapulines, flor de colorín,* and also orchids. I am not ashamed to say that I went from house to house to sell jellies in my town. I also sold *elotes, mangos guamuchil.* In my childhood, even though it was a lot of work, I was very happy, and I also learned to value the sacrifice my parents made to give us what they could.

After finishing high school, I wanted to continue my studies, but my family's economic situation did not allow me to continue with my education. My weighted average in Mexico was 8.3 on average. It wasn't much, but it wasn't too bad either within what would fit in the town where I'm from. In those times, young girls got married very young.

I got married when I was sixteen years old. After two years, I had my first son Carlos. His arrival in my life was the most beautiful thing life could give me. Thank God that I was able to be a mother. The situation with my husband financially was not bad, but we also lived paycheck to paycheck, and his work salary sometimes was not enough. Two years later, we had our second child, another blessing. Thank God for giving me another opportunity to be a mother again. I adore and love my children very much. At that time, the situation was more difficult when there was not enough money, and I had to ask for a loan. After a while, my son, the youngest, needed surgery, and in Mexico, if you did not have the money to pay or did not have medical insurance, they did not treat a patient.

We had to get money and interest. To pay that money, my husband had to decide to come to the United States. He had no choice. He was able to pay the loan after eight months. He later had us join him back in the US. We wanted our children to have the opportunity to have a different life than the one we lived. When we arrived, everything was more challenging. We faced difficult times; one of my children at that time was four years old and the other two years old.

It took a few months for me to find a job. I went to an employment office, and the first day I applied, they sent me to a factory, a printing press. They taught me how to operate a machine where I worked for a few months.

I worked for McDonald's for fifteen years in three restaurants with different owners. In one, I worked for six years, another for seven years, and another for three years. I really liked what I did in my job, and although sometimes the atmosphere among the employees was not very good, I learned to cope with it.

At McDonald's, I worked in the kitchen preparing the salads, the meat, the pies, and yogurts. Sometimes they would put me to fry the potatoes. Other times I was in the drive-thru. I enjoyed working at McDonald's. The work environment was good; we all had a good relationship, from the employees to the managers. Also, at McDonald's, I was the trainer. I received a license in sanitation. I had a lot of experience.

Working at McDonald's taught me everything from the kitchen and preparation to building relations and training. I learned so much, but did not learn English. I was there for many years, but the language did not stick.

After my children grew up, my husband worked in a pallet company. I continued working at McDonald's. We were able to save a little money, and we built good credit. Together with my husband's brother and his family, we had the opportunity to get a house.

As time passed, I continued to push my children to study, and what I sometimes told them was to make the most of their education as much as possible, so that tomorrow they would have a better future. Their effort and hard work would pay off. Thank God, they had that opportunity. It was not easy for them because they were not born here, and it is sometimes difficult for an undocumented immigrant.

I saw their frustration and felt a knot in my heart, wanting to cry, but I didn't show it to them. On the contrary, I told them the same thing: do not give up; keep trying. I've observed that some young people have the opportunity and don't take advantage of it. I am very proud of my children because, despite obstacles, they persisted and never gave up. Carlos, my eldest son, studied at Arrupe College of Loyola. Carlos also studied in Washington, DC, at Georgetown University, where he studied government. My son Israel studied nursing at Malcolm X College. Israel continues his studies at University of Illinois at Chicago (UIC). Both of my sons are independent and have jobs. I could not be prouder of my boys. Carlos works for a company, Civic Consulting Alliance, and Israel works at Advocate Trinity Hospital.

When President Obama granted that young people could obtain DACA, we took advantage of that opportunity. We also continued working and saved a little more. We had the idea of investing, and since my husband had worked in pallets, he knew a person who was a truck driver. The gentleman gave him the idea of getting scrap and pallets. My husband could make and repair pallets, and they did business together. My husband was motivated to start a pallet business and got the materials, a small place, and a breaking machine. He started his own pallet company, Luna Pallets.

After a few months, he had to move from that place because, apart from the fact that it was small, the person who rented it disagreed with the noise, so my brother-in-law found a place they rented. My husband visited several other more prominent pallet companies to see if they bought the pallets. Thank God they bought his pallets.

With the money, he later bought a compressor, another breaking machine, and a trailer. After that, a notcher, and shortly after a forklift. Everything was fine at first. He started selling a pallet trip per week, sometimes two trips. But a year later, we had the bad luck that there was a fire and the place burned down. Everything inside the warehouse burned down: the compressor, the machines, and the forklift.

At that time, I was still working at McDonald's. It was something very hard and heartbreaking, what happened to us. We saw the sacrifice and effort we made shattered. Unfortunately, the place was not insured. My husband was very upset. I fell into a deep depression. I couldn't handle what was happening to me because at that time I was going through a bad experience, I had my own personal problems, and seeing how what we had achieved was lost.

I continued working at McDonald's, but by that time, it was no longer the same. I liked my job and what I did, but I felt that I was drowning and locked up. I would arrive late to work, when before I was very responsible. The manager called this to my attention several times, but I didn't care until one day, I got to work, and since I was late, the manager sent me home and told me to fix my problems first because she wasn't going to allow me to continue being late. With the depression that I was facing, I did not care about going to work, so I didn't go back to work anymore.

After two weeks, my husband started taking out the

burned-down machines. They gave him a chance to go for them. Thank God he just had to change the engine. The band saws and machines worked. We had to start over again from the bottom with our pallet company. I joined my husband and also started working with him. We got a place for rent, and from there, we worked hard and put in all of our efforts; there was no other alternative.

There they taught me how to cut boards of different sizes, the pallet stringers, and eventually how to use the notcher. I was not well yet, but at least I already felt a little free. In the end, that was how I started with the business. I learned how to get material for us to work with to build and repair pallets. I called different companies to see if they would buy pallets from us. We worked with several larger pallet companies.

We later started working with Guero's Pallets and family, Martha Razo and her father Agustin Razo. Until now, we continue to work with them, and we are very grateful for them giving us a hand and allowing us to continue working with them. All this time, we are also working with GTO Recycling, and we also thank them for allowing us to work with them.

What I can tell other people is if they have goals, want to get ahead, then take risks.

There is a phrase that says, "he who does not risk does not win." Do not give up, and don't be left with the doubt—what if I had tried it, maybe it would have been good for me, or maybe I wouldn't make it. Business and everything in life has their highs and lows.

There are even times when you want to throw in the towel. Well, I say that because of the experiences that I have gone through or sometimes I keep facing. But there I am at the foot of the canyon, and it can be said so far that we have not abandoned the ship despite the situations. Thank you very much!

My Final Business Diva Word:

PERSIST

ABOUT VERONICA LUNA

Veronica Luna is the owner of Luna Pallets and the mother of two incredible sons, Carlos and Israel. Veronica is working daily to expand her pallet company and improve the pallet industry.

Veronica Luna
Phone: 773-949-0678
lunaveronica531@gmail.com

EXPLORE YOUR DREAMS AND DISCOVER YOUR REALITY!

GABRIELA GÓMEZ

"The best way to predict the future is to create it."
-Abraham Lincoln

Everything starts—let's call it a thought, an idea, or a wish linked to a dream, imagination, or goal—based on ability, a gift, or enjoyment that you love to do. You are making it happen with a decision full of emotions. Do what you love and love what you do—the saying is famous for a reason.

But it's very hard to start it, right? Like everything in the beginning, we don't know how to begin. We don't know what we don't know until we put it in action and make it happen! This is when we find out that we can take a step forward and feels sometimes we are taking many back. But we decide either to persist or resist. This is where our power is put to test.

Let me share with you some things that I have encountered! My story started like this...

I loved looking good and feeling good ever since I was a little girl. I was that little girl that loved transformation and had a very creative mind. As time went by, I became that girl that likes to see people look good and feel good as they look in the mirror. I became interested in the beauty industry, but coming from a traditional Mexican family, the belief was to obtain a four or more-year career. This was what professional success looked like under my family's system of beliefs. And cosmetology, or anything in the beauty industry, was not seen as a recognized and accepted promising career. The beauty industry was not considered a successful career. Due to that, I decided to study accounting and business to be seen as a competent and accepted successful professional. But I realized I did not enjoy it very much. I graduated and found a good job that made me feel I did the right thing. It also made everyone around me proud of me and made them look up to me at the time. At least, that's how I felt and thought.

My interest in the corporate world decreased as time passed, but I decided to make the best of it. In the meantime, I was doing my hobby, which was beauty makeovers, in my free time. I was doing makeup and hair on weekends for friends and family. Just as a simple, enjoyable hobby! But I found inner peace doing what I enjoyed. Until one day, I was invited to join the beauty industry as a professional. Everyone who loved my work inspired me to do makeup and hair. I never thought this could be my career. I decided to go to beauty school and became a licensed cosmetologist while continuing to do what I most enjoyed: beauty.

I continued to update myself in the beauty industry, and as time went by, many doors opened as I persisted in doing what I loved; magical things happened. I was invited to join a school with their team to assist as an instructor and makeup artist at New York Fashion Week.

Soon after, I was hired as a makeup artist and stylist to go to Europe to the dreamland of Paris and Belgium to join beautiful and talented Latin women with stories that inspire around the world. This allowed me to learn more about these countries and stop by Ireland to see what the other side of the Atlantic looks like. It was an exhilarating and wonderful adventure. At this moment, I felt the passion of my mission and realized that when you do what you love, many other doors open, which take you to places you never thought existed and start appearing in your life, and everything starts looking free and clear.

This was when I decided to continue my journey in the beauty industry, update myself, and create a program that everyone who came across me would benefit from. And ta-da, one day, it came to me in a thought my slogan and beauty program "The Art Between the Inside and Outer Beauty" with the sub slogan "Explore and Discover your New Image."

All the puzzle pieces started to come together, and everything made sense. I began to teach makeup in cosmetology schools, private classes, and everywhere I was asked to teach. I did not have boundaries to teach what I knew and loved to do. I became very inspired and happy by doing this. As I saw the transformation and accomplishments of others, it overwhelmed me with happiness. I started to reach

145

out to organizations and wanted to share my passion with people that would like to make this same career and felt lost or just wanted the experience of the makeover. I joined groups of entrepreneurs, conventions of any type, and any event to help me reach out to more people. I remember what someone once told me: "You will find your mission when you know what you enjoy doing the most without getting tired and when you are also willing to do it for free at times."

I came across an international association of educators in beauty. I took a course with them to expand my ability to teach in a better way and was recognized by them and was named director of this society representing the US. This was a wonderful opportunity and a great accomplishment that was not expected. I could not feel more proud of everything I had accomplished with hard work, persistence, and education in such a short time, just by deciding to do what I love the most and discovering my passion.

As time went by, better things continued to happen until the pandemic happened and I had time to stop and reconsider what was next. All the negativity was turned into positivity, and I continued updating myself in the beauty world online. But my dream became bigger as I had more time to myself. I saw the necessity of others and I decided to take more courses that helped with inner beauty and inner peace. This is when I explored and discovered the new image for my brand. I reinforced the Art Between the inner and Outer Beauty! Just like my slogan expresses and transcends. Slowly, business started to open and gave me hope. I opened a studio and concentrated on inside and external beauty. Holistic beauty, body sculpting, skincare, makeup, and style of hair and teaching beauty professionally became my business focus. It was not easy, like everything that starts with your dream and passion without any assurance. I took baby steps from scratch. Always with faith and focus, I continued the growth. I had to relocate as the building sold and took a chance to go elsewhere in the city. I joined one of my book sisters' spa businesses, and at the same time, I was taking care of my own beauty business and continued building my clientele. Then it was the next step going from a studio to a bigger place. New projects are being born as well. I was always expanding my ideas and dreams. I also found that collaborations are a great step into building your career and expanding your knowledge, experience, and focus.

As I write this, I'm getting ready to go to a big beauty event in Costa Rica as the US Director from the International Association of Educators in Beauty, as well as a platform makeup artist representing the US. From there I will fly to Colombia to dictate my holistic beauty course and program, "The Art Between The Inner and Outer Beauty," and continue to update myself in different areas of beauty. I am creating more alliances and projects internationally. Once I return, the new projects will commence.

There's always a chance, possibility, and space to grow and continue our journey. Our free will, mind, and emotions will make our endeavors happen, and many different things become our reality. Knocking at doors to success will lead us to an amazing world of beautiful colors. Life is full of opportunities and possibilities. Taking risks will lead us to our destiny!

My Final Business Diva Words:

DECISIONS and ACTION

We decide to seek them and enter the world of opportunity. We make that big decision based on will, mind, and emotion. Life is based on decision-making and action! What are your decisions today regarding your life, career, and yourself? What is your power? Your present creates your future, and your past created your present, based on your thoughts, decisions, and emotions, especially your willpower, and that's the beauty of life. Bring out all your power inside out to show your bullet-proof BEAUTY and share the amazing gifts that have made you successful with the world.

ABOUT GABRIELA GÒMEZ

Gabriela Gómez has more than ten years of experience in the art of makeup with international certification, a license in cosmetology, and a certification in neurolinguistic programming, among other programs that helped her create the innovative program based on The Art Between The Inner and Outer Beauty, which focuses on learning to see and feel and experience the beauty beyond the external—combining her makeup artistry with aspects of inner beauty with the help of neurolinguistic training. With this innovative program, Gabriela supports her clients with outer beauty and self-love from within. Gabriela is an instructor and beauty trainer as well as director and representative of A.M.E.B. (World Association of Beauty Educators) in the United States.

Gabriela Gómez
Phone: 872-237-7275
Licensed Cosmetologist
Certified International Makeup Artist
Certified Holistic Therapist

ALEJANDRA MORRIS

"The only limits we have are the ones we believe in our mind."

If you learn anything from my story, please know you can accomplish anything you desire.

As I sat across from an immigration official, I knew my life would change forever and my dream of becoming a USA legal resident would become true. As I heard "your case is approved," I felt free—the freedom that any human being deserves and has the right to.

It was a life-changing moment that just happened in March of 2022, a twenty-year-old dream came true. The VAWA (Violence Against Women Act) made this possible. How did I end up as a woman who went through domestic abuse, you may wonder?

It all started in Arandas Jalisco, Mexico, my birth city. We were raised in a rancho called Valle de San Antonio, near

Arandas. My parents owned a grocery store. They were the hardest workers I know. Having constant food on our table was a privilege where we lived. As anyone familiar with the rancho life, especially years ago, will attest, our home had no running water, electricity, or gas to keep warm.

I would never forget all the memories of doing so many chores like carrying our own water to shower. My mother married very young, and found out about my dad's violent behavior and alcoholism very quickly. Feeling hopeless and having no one to help her, she stayed in the relationship.

We were four children out of nine total pregnancies. Five of these resulted in miscarriages due to the stress and violence my mom suffered, along with my older two siblings. My older sister has been resting from the tremendous abuse she faced. She passed away in her early twenties. My older brother fled our home at the age of fourteen years old to come to the US.

I remember when my mom was leaving our home after a fight with my dad. I grabbed as many clothes as I could in a grocery bag to leave with her, but she told me I had to stay home. Looking back, I had the best role models: my mother and sister. They showed me how to still be good to other people, even if life at home was a living hell. My sister always had a smile on her face. She also loved to get dressed up, as I do.

SCHOOL IS COOL

School was a safe and fun place for me. I excelled at it. At the age of eleven, my parents finally had their final fight, in which my mom almost got shot in front of us. Thankfully, the bullet missed her. The relief of finally never having to see those fights was so immense. My mom had to do anything in her power to support us.

It was time for me to continue to go to middle school; however, we would have to move to Arandas to make this possible. My aunt, Juanita, being the most loving and caring woman I will ever meet, offered to house me. My younger brother eventually ended up moving in with us as well. We did not have any relationship with our mom following the passing of my sister. This affected everyone so much. Feeling alone, unloved, and out of place, I wanted to come to the United States with our dad. He made that possible when I was fourteen years old.

LIFE IN THE USA

Coming to this country undocumented was not a concept I was familiar with. The realization of my situation stunned me. My plans to continue with my higher education were almost impossible. Graduating in the top 10 percent of my class from East Aurora High School allowed me to be a recipient of a two-year scholarship at Waubonsee Community College. Unfortunately, work and staying on top of bills had to be my priority at that time. I fell into a deep depression. Shortly after this, I decided to move out of my dad's house. Learning English was a fast process for my brother and me. Within a year and a half, we were transferred from the bilingual program to regular classes in English.

I didn't have any dating experience, so meeting my son's dad was a lifelong lesson I will be thankful for the rest of my life. Becoming pregnant was such a shock. Nonetheless, I also knew I wanted to give my son a loving family and decided to marry his dad. All along, I knew about his alcoholism, but my unwillingness to work through my deep-rooted issues of insecurity and feeling of unworthiness drove me to keep taking him back as my mom did with my dad.

What stuns me is that I used to say I would not tolerate that from a man and I ended up tolerating it a lot. This was a recipe for disaster. My son, Dylan, made me see the magic in life again since the time I was a child. It is thanks to him I am still here. The marriage was not a good situation. He was not a provider nor did he behave in a way our son could look up to.

On the other hand, we were in the worst situation staying together. Many years had to pass for me to understand I could free us from that toxic living situation. Not having enough support from my family was what held me back the most. I also had anxiety and at times depression. I finally understood the terrible effects staying in that household could have on our son. I called the cops one last time and obtained an order of protection. Dylan and I finally had peace. The peace every human has the right to. God will always provide.

In my case, one of my cousins housed us for a couple of months, and then my younger brother was there to help us get back on our feet. Mutual Ground and a church I attended helped me with counseling.

As difficult as it was to face and confront my memories of pain and hopelessness, it was all absolutely worth it. My life experience was given to me for a reason. Feeling sorry does not benefit me at all. We have to choose whether to become bitter or better. I chose better. I chose to live the life my son and I deserve—one of love and gratefulness.

My sister did not have the opportunities I have. She did not have the blessings I had growing up in the same household. She had to endure the worst. I refuse to be ungrateful and take my life for granted. I wish as women we would help one another more often instead of letting our feelings of insecurity get the best of us.

YOU CHOOSE TO BECOME BETTER OR BITTER

Coming back to my true self was a process, and very painful at times. By my true self, I mean asking myself: Who am I now? What do I want? What really makes me happy? What makes me aspire to be a better person every day?

Forgiving others has always been easy for me; however, forgiving myself has been the tougher part. I thankfully have realized all of it had to happen to guide me to a magnificent place. The drive to become a successful entrepreneur led me to experiment in the cleaning industry.

I remember my mom would tell me no when I wanted strawberry shortcake items from the Avon catalog, so at the age of nine, I joined the Avon selling force. Going to all my neighbors' houses was very fun as usual. If I remember correctly, the lady who was my boss moved, and I had no more Avon business to keep hustling.

I had zero professional cleaning experience and was self-taught. The internet can answer all the questions one has, so I dove in headfirst. Covid pushed me to make the decision and start a cleaning business. Having over a year of experience, I will expand my horizons. Making this decision has helped me find a true passion of mine—more on that to come. Regardless of how successful my cleaning business becomes; I applaud myself for having the courage to follow through. Since my college education was paused after becoming pregnant, I am currently finishing what I started.

Business in general can be everything people tell you. I believe as long as you like what you do and keep persisting, you will get to wherever you want to get. Liking what you do is a major factor, in my opinion. Free resources are available in the community, from how to start one to how to grow your business. Mistakes are inevitable and helpful. So many lessons will not be taught in school. We are also meant to face struggles to make us deal with future struggles better.

LIFE AS WE SEE IT

Every day brings new inspiration to keep working toward my dreams. My son is without a doubt my biggest driving force. I know he knows all the love I have for him. My son's father recently passed away on November 14, 2022. I am more determined to always show him love and share with him how special he is. Our family arguments can include who loves each other more. Of course, I tell him I have to win because I created him. Even though I was never told I was loved growing up, I always knew my mom and dad loved me. I am blessed to have a good relationship with my mom. She is still very hard-working. She motivates me to do better. God sent me these humans to bless me.

TIPS FOR OTHER WOMEN

As our women's rights have evolved, so has the pressure to be able to keep up with every area of our lives. I believe it can be done. Instead of trying to be there for everyone and do everything for everyone, I believe in balance, to choose the course of our lives. If that includes becoming a working mom, delegate tasks among family members and hire help if needed.

My mom was always working either at home or the grocery store. She has been a great role model for her work ethic. She is in her sixties and works very hard, and still has the energy to take care of home chores. I have realized that no matter how good you try to be as a woman, you can't please everyone. We are the ones who know what we need and what our family needs. Being a woman and a minority can come with challenges. Nonetheless, eventually, we can accomplish any goal we set. Our children watch everything we do more than what we say.

My Final Business Diva Word:

ASPIRATION

Dream as big as your imagination allows, and then dream bigger the next time. Everything happens for you, not to you. Your dreams and aspirations were given to you; don't expect anyone else to validate it. Failing is part of becoming successful.

You are the creator of your life. Think again about everything you have been taught.

Everything starts with self-love, so work on that first. People who truly love you and are meant to be in your life will remain with you no matter what.

ABOUT ALEJANDRA MORRIS

Alejandra Morris was born and raised in Jalisco, Mexico, until the age of fourteen years old. She is the owner of #It'sclean Cleaning Services LLC in Oswego, Illinois. She started the company in the summer of 2021, after yearning to experiment in the business world. This led her to want to pursue a career in real estate, as well as launching a jewelry line.

Her Roxy Paw Pals nonprofit foundation has fed and neutered homeless dogs and cats in Mexico. As a child, her family housed homeless dogs. Every animal deserves a loving home. We are their voice.

Alejandra received the Gustafson Scholarship from Waubonsee Community College,

John J. Swalec Jr. President's Achievement Award, and other scholarships throughout her college years. She is a member of The National Technical Honor Society, Alpha Beta Gamma Honor Society, and The Society for Collegiate Leadership and Achievement. She is currently finishing her business major at Waubonsee Community College.

The role of being a mom is her favorite one. Dylan Morris is a twelve-year-old boy with a wonderful and kind heart. He loves to play football and catch frogs anywhere he can find them. Being a mom has made her world one of so much magic and love.

Alejandra Morris

Phone: 630-677-6887

IG: @alejandramorrisgarcia

FB: Alejandramorris

LinkedIn: @Alejandra Morris

claudiamorris87@gmail.com

A DESTINED PATH: MY JOURNEY

ELIZABETH VILLARREAL

"You must be uncomfortable to be comfortable."

I remember when I was ten years old, and I asked my father if I could start my own business selling *raspas* (snow cones). I told him I wanted a little store in the front yard where my customers could walk up to my stand and ring the bell to buy my raspas. I was daddy's little girl, so he agreed, and hired someone to build a tiny room outside our front yard by the fence. My dad painted the raspa stand white, and I can still see his handwriting at the top of my business. He wrote, "Lizzy's Snow Cones."

It looked like a tiny shed room, and it barely fit two people, just enough for my mom and I to make the raspas. I remember my brothers making fun of it and calling it an outhouse. I didn't care; I was so proud of my little raspa stand. I was making money. They weren't laughing at me when they needed money to borrow on weekends. Ha!

I remember my mom had the little bank bag full of money, and it made me feel rich! I imagine it wasn't very much, and probably mostly the change she got for me to have on hand. The feeling and the power it gave me to have my own money was amazing. This was a huge lesson for me, especially when we didn't have much. For the first time in my young life, I had the power to make my own money, and it felt good. I realize now, my parents were my first mentors that supported their ten-year-old daughter to open her first business. That was the beginning of my entrepreneurship.

I was born in Chicago, but at the age of five years old my mom and two older brothers moved back to our hometown of Laredo, Texas, in the '70s, which is a small border town, where I lived for thirty years of my life.

My father died when I was thirteen years old, and my mom became a single mom. At the time, it was just her and I left in the house. My two older brothers had left the house, and I can say it was a difficult time for us. My mom was so strong, and I never saw her cry or complain of her struggles. My mother was tough, and she would be the first to tell you to stop complaining and get back to work. No use crying when it still must get done. I realize now, I am my mother's child.

My mother purchased my very first car at the age of sixteen, I can still remember, a white Ford Fairmont with red interior. It was a beauty! I didn't want to incur another burden on my mom, so I started working at McDonald's immediately.

I was a very outgoing, busy teen, and kept myself busy with school, work, and at that time I was the captain of the color-guard, my junior and senior year. That was a part-time job, between making up the routines for the songs during marching season and teaching the sixteen girls I had to lead. Looking back now, I had such a huge responsibility at such a young age. This molded me to be a confident, strong leader.

The band directors that I had at the time were very strict and expected the best from us and nothing less. What was asked was expected to be done. This taught me discipline and determination to succeed. The repetitions of the routines and learning them over and over until they were perfect provided the strong will and determination that has guided me throughout my life and career.

Try and try again until you succeed. That is a very important lesson in life that I have learned. There is no success unless you fail. Success does not come easy; it will take intense labor, sweat, and tears. Oh boy, have I cried, and I remember my mom telling me, "There is nothing you cannot do, Liza."

Leaders continue working toward their goals no matter how difficult they may be. Ask yourself, do I easily get discouraged and give up on myself, or am I stubborn until I succeed?

I never realized how poor we were until I look back now at my childhood. Looking at the pictures of my home then, I remember thinking I had the ugly orange house on the block. My father brought leftover orange paint from his construction job and decided to paint our cinder block home orange. It wasn't regular paint, because when you'd get close or lean on it, it was all over your clothes. I can laugh about it now, but at the time, I was so embarrassed by my bright orange home. Looking at me now, you would never think I came from such a humble beginning. Having very little growing up has made me extremely driven to take my son and me to the next level.

I recently saw a picture of myself from when I was about six years old in my backyard, and there were chickens in the background. I was wearing my long red dress with white lace my mom had made for me. There was my slide in the background, the steel slide that burned my buns many times in that Texas heat. It brought so many memories of me playing in the backyard by myself. When I look back at those pictures, it is easy to forget where I came from. I know that is what gave me the drive to work hard. I may not always think I have accomplished much, but I know my son now has what I never had growing up.

We tend to focus on what we don't have rather than on what we do have, and everything we have accomplished. I have gotten into the habit of writing down everything I have accomplished. This is when you can see all your lifetime achievements. I thank God for all the blessings he has given me. I recommend sitting down once a year and writing down all that you have accomplished in your life.

This will give you a better perspective and appreciation of where you come from to where you are now. Then write down everything you want to accomplish moving forward. Get into the habit of looking at your accomplishments and goals year after year, and you will see more is accomplished than what you give yourself credit for.

When I was twenty-eight years old, I had my little bundle of joy, Robert Alexander. I remember buying baby books to find the perfect name. I wanted a powerful, strong name. God knew I needed a strong boy to be by my side as I entered my new chapter as a single mom—the most rewarding job in my life.

At that time, I was working at an office as an office manager, and as a part-time personality on the radio. Working in radio helped me be able to speak in front of people and not be shy. Working as an on-air personality is all unplanned, and you must make it up as you go. You are entertaining people and must be the life of the party as you sit alone in that tiny room. The only disadvantage of working in radio in a smaller city where everyone knows everyone is that everyone knows everyone. That was a bit creepy for me when people thought they knew me. As a single mom, that was the attention I did not want.

While working one of my shifts on the radio, my boss and owner of the radio station asked me if I wanted a job in sales, not realizing I had a day job. He said, "You have a great personality; it is good for sales." At the same time, my best friend Olivia was working at Southwestern Bell Wireless, and she was talking about an opening they had in outside sales.

I had never done sales, and I was not that thrilled about it. She assured me I would do great, and it had the potential to make great money. It paid $13,500 base plus commission. I was making 30K with overtime, which was significantly more than the 13k they were offering. I had people advising me that sales were unpredictable, and not a steady income.

I remember asking a peer, Jorge, who worked in radio sales. He said the possibility to make great money was there. What is great money? How much do you make with commission? With a 13K salary? Are you kidding me? I was a single mother, and I knew I wanted more for my son. I knew that if I wanted a better life to provide for my son, I had to take a leap of faith and do what I didn't want to do—and that was sales. The obvious decision for me at the time was a reputable company. It was Southwestern Bell; what can go wrong?

My son was five months old at the time of my career change, and he is turning twenty-three in a few months—and I now have twenty-three years of experience in business sales. It was the best decision of my life. It allowed me to raise my son on one income. The good news was in the second month of starting at SBC, the company doubled the salary. WOW!! That was God's blessing! I didn't know anything about mobile phones or sales. I had a six-month-old to support and I started knocking at businesses selling.

Mobile phones were still new in 2000, so convincing businesses to get phones instead of radios was not easy. In six months, I made more money than I had made in my whole life. I am blessed I took a leap of faith to do something I was not comfortable doing. I never saw myself doing sales, but I can't imagine where my life would be if I didn't take that leap of faith.

That brings me to another important lesson in life. Sometimes in life, we must do what is uncomfortable to lead comfortable lives. In my life, this was business sales. I was able to raise my son on one income.

I am the youngest of nine children. My father was disabled, and my mom worked as a custodian in an elementary school during the week, and at nights and weekends, she sold Avon, Tupperware, Stanley, and sometimes homemade dolls.

My mom worked twice as hard to make sure we never were without anything. My mom did not drive at the time, and I remember walking in the Texas heat to do Tupperware parties and deliver the customers' orders. Before she died, I remember my mom told me, "You learned sales from me, from helping me when you were a little girl." You sure did teach me, Mom. Thank you, *Mami!*

My mother was my very first mentor as an entrepreneur. My mother had a third-grade education, but she was the most intelligent woman I have ever met. She taught herself to speak, read, and write English when they moved to Chicago. She never believed she was smart, but she would run circles around many intelligent people. She was never afraid to speak the truth. I think I get that from her.

I see it now, my mom struggling, and I am sure she did not want to walk blocks and blocks dragging me with her in the heat after a long day at work. I thought it was fun, plus I got to get cakes or cookies, whatever they would serve. She did what she had to do to provide for us. She taught me you must work hard even if I may not always want to do it.

During the pandemic, I was selling skincare and makeup virtually part-time with a company called Senegence. I was able to make enough money on nights and weekends to pay off my car. I met some amazing ladies that taught me how to market using social media, and I learned how to put on makeup. We did virtual parties using Facebook. It was an entirely different virtual world. It was an amazing experience. Sometimes we must work a little extra hard when money is tight.

When I was in my twenties, I started reading books about finance, and I was trying to teach myself everything I could about finance. I didn't want to struggle like my parents did. I wanted to learn how to retire rich! I'm not there yet, obviously, but I taught myself enough to be blessed to have the choice to retire in four years.

I wanted to work in finance as a financial advisor, educate myself, and help people learn about finance and to save for retirement. When my son was eleven years old, I was really thinking about going into it, but I realized this was a job with commission only. As a single mother, I did not have the luxury to gamble on changing careers with no salary.

I wanted to teach those that do not have the money to pay for financial advice. There is a need to educate people on how to save for their retirement and prepare for their future. There is a major misconception that you need a lot of money. You don't, and I know my parents didn't know that. This was one leap of faith I was not determined to do. If I can go back in time, I would take that job and take the leap of faith. And believe in myself that I could succeed.

I'm now in the next chapter of my life. It is never too late to start another career. I recently got engaged to a wonderful man named Eduardo. He and I have recently started our own business in finance. The next chapter is about bringing financial literacy to our Latino culture. We are both blessed with great careers, and now we find the need to pay it forward.

It is exciting to start a new career together with a partner that supports you. It is never too late to start a second career, and even a third as we have. We started our real estate endeavor, and in honor of my mother Ramona, we named it MonaLiza Investments, LLC, which we started in 2022.

I believe if you believe in yourself or have someone by your side to support you, the possibilities are endless. I have been blessed to find a wonderful man in my life now that supports me in everything I do. He jumps right in with me in my endeavors. He gives me the confidence that my mom always did growing up. My mom left us in November 2020, but I know she is with me every step guiding me.

We may not be where we want to be, but we are working at it every day to make it happen.

Here are key rules I have always lived by:

- If you don't start, you will never succeed.
- Never let failure keep you from succeeding.
- "The road to success and the road to failure are on the same road."—Unknown
- Don't be afraid to get uncomfortable to get things done.
- Take risks!

My Final Business Diva Word:

GET UNCOMFORTABLE!

Our paths in life are never easy. Life has taught me that I had to get uncomfortable with jobs I may not have wanted to take, but it has led me to where I am today, raising my son on a one-income household to provide a better life. Go get uncomfortable!

ABOUT ELIZABETH VILLARREAL

Elizabeth Villarreal was a Client Solution Executive with AT&T for 21 years. She received her bachelor's degree in marketing. She is an Author, Entrepreneur, Financial Professional, and proud mom of twenty-two-year-old son, Robert. She served as board member on multiple Latino nonprofit organizations. She is passionate about mentoring, inspiring young leaders, and working with women to dream again. Dreams and goals are attainable, which starts with believing in yourself. "Getting uncomfortable to be comfortable." Her mission is to change the trajectory of Latino families by teaching financial literacy and help build generational wealth.

Elizabeth Villarreal
LizaLove.latina@gmail.com

BLESSED

SUSAN ALBERGO VAZQUEZ

"Inhale Passion, Exhale Fear"

Seriously, I wasn't supposed to be here at all. My mother had gone to have me aborted sixty-four years ago. She was waiting her turn at the clinic and waiting, until she decided to leave and come back on a different day. Since you are reading this, you know she never did go back! I thank God that she never went back. I believe that what the enemy meant to kill, God uses for good for those who choose to follow Him.

I was born on the day my father and godfather opened the doors to Little Joe's Famous Pizza on 63rd St & Richmond in Chicago. The grand opening took place on September 19, 1958. I was the firstborn and had one brother arrive six years later.

Growing up, my father would say to me more times than I would have liked to hear, "How come you weren't the boy?" (I believe the Italians took pride in their firstborn being a boy.) And, I would tell him, because I am NOT! I was pretty laid back; most times, I would let it roll off my back. However, I believe that "played" in my self-consciousness. I wanted to please my father more because I wasn't the boy. I had ambition and drive and tried to make him proud of me.

Many things came easy for me. We had a great life, and I lacked for nothing. Vacationing for me started at a year old going on my first plane ride to Florida. My father and mother would take us at least once or twice a year on vacations, mostly to Florida. As a side note, how coincidental that I am sitting now writing this and tweaking the rest of this story in Florida, and Hurricane Ian is pounding at my balcony door, and the rain is pelting!

I came to Ft. Lauderdale a few days early, even though people were evacuating the state. My children were questioning my motives for going into such a storm. I had a business convention to attend on the weekend. And I had my faith! I believed that God would keep me safe. I seriously had peace and calm about me going. For a minute, when I was boarding the plane, I started questioning myself...but there were other crazy people right along with me, and the flight was pretty full, right?! I then asked the flight attendant, "Did many people cancel on this flight?"

She responded, "No, not really, but I am surprised we are STILL going to take off, since there are so many storms in Ft. Lauderdale!"

I did start to think at that moment, *What am I doing?* Only for a moment! I felt the Lord answer me about fifteen minutes after take-off, with a MOST GLORIOUS SUNRISE! I took pictures and wish this book could have pictures. It took my breath away, and I felt such peace!

I remember begging my father to let me work the cash register around the age of twelve. He got tired of me asking for the next two years (the squeaky wheel gets the oil), and he finally let me start training when I turned fourteen. I was on the phone, taking customers' orders and learning how to count money back and give change. To this day, I never let the cash register think for me. I could push a couple of extra buttons for the register to TELL ME how much change I need to return, but I prefer not to. It is good to keep your mind sharp and think for YOURSELF on your feet. I also remember how grueling it was when my father trained me to count the change back. He had no patience with me, and the tears flowed along with the frustration, until the formula kicked in, which was exciting! I FINALLY understood, and, even to this day, it makes me smile when I step in to give a customer their change.

Some things sound so basic, but I am sure you have heard the saying, "Get back to basics!" It's so true, right? Another basic fact my father told me was to NEVER put the money away in the register before giving back the change. I did forget sometimes, and a couple of those times, the customer would say they gave me a bigger bill and accuse me of giving back incorrect change. After checking into it, they would apologize to me for being an inconvenience.

(There will always be someone wanting to take advantage of a situation.) Throughout your life, there will be "givers" and "takers," and that is just a fact of life! Always strive to be a giver; give always and it will always return to you tenfold!

Growing up through the years with the restaurant, many regular customers became like *familia!* Many would tell stories about me dancing in front of the jukebox as a little girl. (Dance like no one is watching!) And sitting at the table with customers sharing their French fries or pizza. "Ala nostra tavola si mangia sempre bene" is an Italian proverb that means "At our table, one always eats well." I grew up at a great time on the South Side of Chicago and I loved talking to our customers.

I went to Southwest School of Business and completed that course after graduating from Mother McAuley Liberal Arts High School. My first job out of that school was with a small law firm. I became a legal secretary. This was very different from moving all around at the restaurant. Can you imagine, I had to sit at a desk, answer phones, and type all day? This was very different for me. I felt important and I liked being needed to get the work done! However, it was hard for me to sit in one place very long. This was a smaller law firm with only two attorneys (husband & wife), myself, and another secretary. There were few people to talk with, since I was used to dealing with many people at once and a more "hopping" environment. (I believe I was a people pleaser, so it was easier for me to follow the rules.)

After a few years with this law firm, my best friend and I quit our jobs to go to sunny Florida. We stayed a few months at my father's condo in Hallandale. A couple of young girls having lots of fun in the sun but guess what? I ran out of money, and my friend did not. Well, I walked down to a local Italian restaurant my father used to bring me to called Jimmy Di Nicola's Grist Mill. I asked to speak with the owner Jimmy, and he interviewed me. The only opening was for a server. Wait, what?? I couldn't serve! I was terrified to carry any trays of food. That is why I never even served at our own restaurant. I was very comfortable on the phone. Well, I took the job because I needed money and I loved the atmosphere and great food, and he offered it to me. It doesn't matter if you are scared...DO IT ANYWAY! What is your WHY? Your WHY needs to make you CRY, and you will move forward to get it!

Do you know how big their trays were to carry compared to the trays at our restaurant? DOUBLE the size! I won't lie; I was super freaking out. However, I had great teammates who showed me, encouraged me, and helped me with those huge trays. Because they showed me and encouraged me, I, too, always want to encourage others to do whatever they put their minds to do. Kindness goes a long way, and I will never forget how they made me feel!

In the meantime, my father and godfather decided to sell their (our) restaurant at the end of 1990. I never did tell you that I had met my husband in that restaurant (both of them). Ha-ha, seriously! My first husband and I entertained on cruise ships doing a comedy-magic act and traveling the world. I had seen more of the world by the age of twenty-three than most people ever will. However, we had some issues, and long story, we ended up getting divorced and not having any children.

My second husband was the chef at Little Joe's, and I hopped out of the fire into the frying pan (no pun intended). We have been married thirty-seven years now and have three beautiful grown children and two grandchildren.

So, my father, chef husband, brother, and I all became partners and opened our next Little Joe's in Tinley Park, Illinois. We bought our first home close to the original restaurant on 63rd Street on 57th & Lawndale. It's important to know that if you are going into business with a partner, make sure you are evenly yoked! I can NOT stress this enough. Maybe that makes you think, well, that is only in marriage; however, if you have a partner, it's pretty much the same as being married! Also, do NOT get comfortable in your business. I made that mistake and lost thousands of dollars! I thought everyone was "watching out for it," but it is NOT their business, and nobody will care like the owners. After buying out my father, we proceeded to open seven more restaurants, but that is a story for another book!

I always knew there was a more innovative, better way to work; work smarter and not harder! Whether you own your own business or have a job or profession, I learned it's wise to have multiple income streams. While working full-time downtown and helping the restaurant, I got introduced to direct sales. At first, I didn't want to learn about it. I was turned off by one of our servers that was ALWAYS trying to sell me something, and shove Jesus down my throat. She was so pushy, I couldn't take it, and she wouldn't take NO for an answer.

I did wind up getting involved in direct sales and I found so much positive mindset there, and then guess what? At a convention, I found Jesus Christ. At a Sunday morning, nondenominational service, the pastor was talking RIGHT TO ME! Tears flowed, and I went to give my heart to Jesus at the altar call. This is priceless, and I have been drawing closer to Him since that beautiful experience. I give Him the glory because with Him, all things are possible! That was years ago, and I'm proud to say I am currently with a wonderful company that allows me to help others make and save money as well.

Life is short and goes by oh so fast. When I was asked to be in this wonderful book with such fabulous Business Divas, I asked myself why I wanted to do this. I have never authored a book. I asked the Lord and told Him, I want to help and encourage other women to pursue their dreams, and if I can help them, then I am so glad to do that. Also, to inspire them to seek Jesus Christ and ask Him to be their Lord and Savior. Life is so much better following His ways than our own. I am so grateful to be alive, as I could have been dead for so many stupid things I did. I wish I could go back and redo some things. However, I believe everything happens for a reason, and I know, without a shadow of a doubt, that Jesus was watching over me. No matter what situation you are in, call out to Jesus. One of my favorite verses is Proverbs 3:5–6. Trust in the Lord with all your heart and lean not on your own understanding; in all your ways submit to Him, and He will make your paths straight!

My Final Business Diva Word:

REJOICE

Going into a business can create so many emotions and has many ups and downs. There are many days I want to cry about one thing or another. And some days, I do. But God...I turn to Him and thank Him. It is amazing when you start counting your blessings, your troubles melt away. Reminds me of a verse in First Thessalonians 5:16–18 Rejoice always, pray continually, give thanks in all circumstances; for this is God's will for you in Christ Jesus. We are all on a journey, and some struggle more than others. If you are following Christ, He will help you. Ask Him to show you what is next. I ask Him daily.

Wishing You
all of the
Season's Best

FIRST NATIONAL
BANK OF BROOKFIELD

THIS IS YOUR RECEIPT

WHEN MAKING A DEPOSIT AT A TELLERS WINDOW, ALWAYS OBTAIN AN OFFICIAL RECEIPT.
Checks and other items are received for deposit subject to the provisions of
the Uniform Commercial Code or any applicable collection agreement.

FDIC

ABOUT SUSAN ALBERGO VAZQUEZ

Susan is a multiple business owner and entrepreneur, and now a first-time author. She is a proud mother of three beautiful grown children, Gerardo, Vincenzo, and Victoria, and two precious grandchildren, Braven and Harmony. She has been busy running two Italian restaurants and the day-to-day operations that come with the territory.

She almost did not contribute, as she felt overwhelmed with life and had too much on her plate. Since she has a passion for helping other women, she decided to accept the challenge and encourage others to embrace their calling.

Susan started working at age fourteen in the family restaurant and has been involved in her family business for over sixty years. She has also worked in many other capacities such as a legal secretary, an administrative assistant, Midway Airlines, and even a magician's assistant entertaining on cruise ships. Susan believes that even when you find your passion, whether owning a business, or working a 9–5, having multiple streams of income & building a residual income is very important!

Susan Albergo Vazquez
suzivaz1@gmail.com
FB: SuziQ's Passion Unlimited / @SuziQsPassions
IG: @SuziVaz1

ELIUTH GUZMAN

"Haz lo que te apasione y persigue tus sueños."

CHICAGO, MY NEW LIFE

My name is Eliuth Guzman. I was born in Mexico City. When I was three years old, my father left for the United States, seeking a better life for our family. It took eight long years for my family to be together again.

I arrived in Chicago when I was eleven years old. I was too young to understand how far we were from our country, Mexico, but I knew that after several years, we would finally be back together as a family.

As I was the youngest, my elder sister made sure that my only priority was school. My siblings had to work hard and make many sacrifices with my parents so that I would have a better future. They were clear that education could offer me better opportunities.

I was always very fond of school. It was very difficult at first because I did not speak or read English, but I learned it very quickly. I graduated from grammar school with honors, I finished high school with honors, and I had the opportunity to attend college because I received several scholarships that helped cover my education.

ACHIEVING ALL MY PROFESSIONAL GOALS

In the last year of high school, when I had to decide what I would study, I took a journalism class, and only after some weeks, I was the editor for my high school magazine. When I took this class, I fell in love with it, and I realized I had to study something related to the media.

In 2001, I got my bachelor's degree in marketing communications from Columbia College, Chicago. This was one of my first accomplishments that made my family proud, as I was the first one to receive a university degree. Three years after graduation, I achieved one of my most desired goals: to work in the field of my profession. I had the opportunity to work for the *Chicago Tribune* for ten years in the *Hoy* newspaper, the Spanish edition. I started as an assistant to the national sales department, climbing up to become the supervisor of the classifieds sales department. Being part of the *Chicago Tribune* has been one of the best experiences in my life, and where I met the most incredible people who were my great mentors in the communications industry.

CHOOSING THE BUSINESS PATH

While working for the *Chicago Tribune,* I had the idea to start my own business in the food industry. I started Latin Plate Catering & Events, a company that offers food service, waiters, decorations, and event planning. I had no experience of how to start a business, but I did research on the events industry for the Latino community with a focus on *quinceañeras* (A *quinceañera* is a celebration of a girl's fifteenth birthday).

The results were fantastic. As Latinos, we love to celebrate all special occasions, and the Quinces party is full of our Hispanic culture and traditions. I found out there was a big opportunity to start my catering and event planning services for this market.

One day, I was invited to a small Quince Expo in a banquet hall. I was very excited to be at the expo, and started to create a company name, logo, menu package, and business cards. Attending my first expo helped me get my first clients. I was very nervous about planning my first event because it was a big responsibility to plan or provide a service for a special occasion for the clients. They trusted me in their special event, and there is only one opportunity to make it right. This day I found my passion, where I could put into practice my experience in marketing, sales, and customer service that I had been gathering for more than ten years.

In 2018, I decided to leave the corporate world to devote myself full-time to Latin Plate Catering. It was a very difficult decision because I did not have any experience as an entrepreneur, but I trusted in this project and decided to take the risk. It was not easy at all to make my way into the events industry, yet all along this way, I met incredible people who believed in me and allowed me to coordinate their special events. The most gratifying thing was at the end of each event, when the clients were happy with our food and event-planning services. That encouraged me to continue the entrepreneurship journey. My main goal for each event is for the client to enjoy their special occasion.

GROWTH OF LATIN PLATE CATERING & EVENTS

After several years of rendering our services to the Hispanic community planning *quinceañeras*, weddings, and birthday parties, my next goal was to bring my services to corporate companies in the city of Chicago. It was in 2019 when I entered into an association that would open the doors for me to serve lunches to the best companies in Chicago, such as the Willis Tower building. With this opportunity, we had an unimaginable growth: we were preparing one thousand lunches per week, and we obtained recognition from our clients as the best Latin food. We had a busy year, and were hired to serve the Christmas dinner for Chicago Mayor Lori E. Lightfoot and her staff. It was an honor to be part of this prestigious event.

REINVENTING MYSELF AS A BUSINESSWOMAN DURING THE PANDEMIC

Latin Plate was vanishing in front of my eyes; a job of more than twelve years had completely been brought to a halt by the Covid-19 pandemic. Those were very difficult months; I had no idea how I could survive financially, since my only source of income was the catering.

When I found out that the government would provide assistance to small businesses, I filled out lots of applications, with the hope of receiving some kind of support to be able to pay the rent for my commercial kitchen, because I knew that if I lost it, I would no longer have a place to continue preparing the food. It was frustrating not to receive any response, and I realized that there was a clear inequality between small and minority-owned companies.

My business coach Rowan Richards from Allies for Community Business organization continued to encourage me not to give up, and soon the answers from the grants began to arrive. At that time, I knew I had to innovate, since there was no scheduled date for the offices and events to return to normal activities. In the midst of a pandemic, I decided to open my long-awaited healthy café and protein bar. I went back to the neighborhood where I grew up in Wicker Park to open the healthy café and protein bar. Focused on "guilt-free" protein-based snacks, protein-packed coffees, and antioxidant-rich supplement smoothies and teas, World Nutrition filled a gap in the Wicker Park area.

In August 2020, I found the perfect place. For two nonstop, tiring months, I hired professional workers to build the place, and on Saturday, October 10, 2020, it was the grand opening. The café replaced a Jimmy John's, and the Alderman Daniel La Spata was extremely happy to support our business. He attended the ceremony and did the honor of cutting the ribbon for the grand opening. This day was filled with emotions, as I was achieving a dream of having my first brick-and-mortar business location. I was also nervous because we were in a community to serve the Anglo market and, as a Latina, I did not know what the reaction would be, but I was pleasantly surprised to have all the support of the community as they gave me a warm welcome. This is a very lively community. They take care of themselves. They go running, exercise, and go for long walks. I love and enjoy what I do so much that it does not feel like work; besides, we are also helping people with healthier alternatives for their daily routine.

I am the first woman in my family to start a business and now run a cafe. Without a doubt, I owe this success to my family, my friends, to all the people who have guided me in my professional career, and now in the business world, especially to my husband, business partner and executive chef, Omar Guzman, who with his great culinary talent has created a variety of dishes for each of our clients in the catering and now in the new protein bars.

COMPANY GROWTH AND EXPANSION

These last two years have not been easy for my companies because it was like starting over from scratch during the pandemic, but staying focused on the growth goal has been important.

In 2022, I obtained one of the most important food contracts with the Obama Foundation, delivering thirty-five thousand fresh-cooked meals for children in summer camps. We also expanded with new protein bars in new communities. My passion for food goes beyond generating income. I provide jobs and fill a gap by providing healthy and fresh food options for our customers and the communities in Chicago.

MY MOST IMPORTANT ROLE: BEING A MOTHER

I have the fortune of being a mom of three amazing children. The first, Montserrat, who is twenty years old, is pursuing her bachelors at DePaul University in Chicago. I have always taught her about the importance of education to achieve all her goals. My second daughter, Dayanara, fifteen, is a very dedicated student, always with honors, and she is currently in tenth grade. The youngest, Giancarlo, twelve, came to complete my family and filled me with lots of love. He is very talented at drawing.

My first step in events was planning my children's birthdays. I still remember planning amazing birthday celebrations for them. Of course, I could not miss the quince party for my eldest daughter; it was a magical event created for a queen.

My Final Business Diva Word:

PASSION

"All Our Dreams Can Come True
If we have the courage to pursue them." —Walt Disney

We are all capable of achieving our dreams and we have great talents and abilities; the most important thing is to be able to do what we are passionate about and be willing to work hard to achieve them.

It will not be easy.

It will be many hours of work,

some days you'll want to give up,

but the satisfaction of seeing it come true is priceless.

ABOUT ELIUTH GUZMAN

Eliuth Guzman is an entrepreneur with more than fifteen years in the food industry. She is the founder and CEO of Latin Plate Catering & Events Corp, Cofounder of World Nutrition, Owner of Dream Nutrition Café, and Coauthor of *Today's Inspired Latina IX.*

While pursuing a successful career in corporate sales organizations, the idea of starting her own business took hold. So, twelve years ago, she took the leap. But it was in 2018 that she decided to commit full-time to Latin Plate.

Latin Plate has allowed her to combine her passion and expertise in event planning, sales, and customer service. Originally, she began the catering business within the Hispanic community by catering to weddings, cotillions, and birthdays. But she had a broader vision and wanted to provide services and of course, food, to a wider market.

In 2020, she opened her first brick-and-mortar café/ protein bar in the Wicker Park community, offering delicious desserts and foods but with a healthy twist. In 2022, she opened her second café/protein bar in Edgewater community. She looks forward to continuing to grow the catering business, plans to keep expanding her brand café/ protein bar, and pursuing an MBA in Business Administration.

She has earned several recognitions and awards as a professional and entrepreneur. Eliuth was invited to have dinner with President Obama to celebrate the progress of the Presidential Center.

Eliuth Guzman

Latin Plate Catering & Events Corp

eliuth@latinplatecatering.com

FB: Latin Plate Catering

IG: @Latinplate

World Nutrition Cafe

2029 W Division St

Chicago IL 60622

FB: World Nutrition Smoothie and Juice Bar

IG: @Worldnutritionchi

Dream Nutrition Cafe

6206 N Broadway

Chicago IL 60660

FB: Dream Nutrition Cafe

IG: @DreamNutrition

LIZ QUINTANA ROMERO

"What you are is God's gift to you, what you become is your gift to God."

My family comes from El Estado De Mexico, Mexico, from a little town called Santa Maria La Loma. It's a town surrounded by mountains and peace. You can find beautiful humble souls and the best comfort food there. Whenever I visit, it reminds me of how the world is bigger than our small ups and downs. Traveling overall does that for me. As a travel fanatic, I write this as I'm up in the air on my way to a women's retreat in Guadalajara, Mexico.

My family's hometown is dear to my heart. They decided to immigrate to the US to be able to provide a better life for us when they planned a family. They chose the east side of

Aurora, IL, as the area is rich with immigrants, and we helped each other grow and settle and adjust faster.

Aurora, IL, has done so much for me; it molded me into the woman I am becoming. Just like my small town in Mexico, growing up, East Aurora was a town of humble families working to make a better life. I know that seeing all of my hard-working people achieve greatness has impacted me so much, and I look up to people like Dolores Huerta.

I obtained my bachelor's degree in social services at Lewis University. I always wanted to pursue higher education. Education for me is important, regardless of the major or how many degrees. I think being a woman and educated elevates us, no matter what role we end up in life.

I did not end up continuing because of the debt that comes with acquiring an education. I was blessed to have scholarships for my undergrad that allowed me to now have no more school debt. I knew pursuing my master's would mean more debt and also delay me in being able to become a homeowner, something I dreamed of early on. So, I had to decide which debt I wanted: a master's or a mortgage. I chose the mortgage because I knew that this investment would provide me with the stability I wanted at that time.

As soon as I graduated, I became a foster case worker and then I switched to HR. I wanted to be a counselor. I always knew I wanted to help people. I wanted to focus on working with youth, specifically at a detention center. My motive was to help the kids that needed help the most or who are sometimes left behind. I wanted to help them before their life circumstances were even more difficult.

My first job was at a foster care center; I started as an intern in college, and then later I was hired. I always knew I wanted to do more, but I felt it was not enough. I was always searching for how to help others more deeply. Next, I went into HR, which was more for the facility, since foster care involves a lot of travel. The HR position was also at a more stable location. I was now able to help others to get a job. I ended up not liking it, though; I wanted to help people. Working with people in a district limited whom I could help.

During the pandemic, I had to work remotely. I saw firsthand the inequalities that were discussed so much that year and always knew that some of us were behind with things, opportunities like financial literacy, homeownership, and knowing how to build wealth with real estate.

This really opened my eyes to connect the pieces on what I was searching for; purpose to get up to work toward each day, while indeed making a huge impact. I spoke to a friend about what was happening and realized that by working together and helping others financially, I can make an impact.

I know I can make an impact in people's lives because I ensure that my clients understand what they are buying and what they are paying for, and if they will still be able to afford necessities or live comfortably. My parents had rental properties, and I knew how buying a home could set someone in a better place financially and provide stability and security. So, my purpose in life is to continue to guide those who choose to work with me, to make sure they are winning when they buy a home.

FIRST BUSINESS EXPERIENCE

I did research first; I had to take a mortgage lending class at a school. To pass the class and the final exam, I had to take the state test that is timed at a testing center. Once I passed that, I was licensed with what they call an NMLS. Right after receiving my license, I had to look for a company to sponsor me.

Now I work with the #1 team in FHA Lending in IL, and #2 in the region, being the #1 lender for the Federal Housing Administration (FHA). Making sure that I'm able to provide people with the best is important because I know I am completing my purpose. As a mortgage queen, I will continue to do so by continuing to learn every single day and find new opportunities and growth in my career so that I can better serve the people that pick me as their mortgage advisor.

It has been a great experience knowing the people and communities I serve. For example, if a client doesn't have citizenship or is the first in their family to buy a home, we offer loan solutions. We know how to help everyone, and I can make a bigger impact. We are supposed to be lenders; we have to provide equal services and be able to help everyone. I have realized that some mortgage companies do not entirely educate themselves to serve all people. Becoming a lender for me was to provide equal housing and to guide people to a better place than they were before when making a home purchase.

I've learned that there is still so much work to be done as a young Business Diva who is constantly thinking of new ways and opportunities to make an impact in my community.

There are many mortgage companies and real estate brokers in the state, but there is only one me. I have a passion for making an impact in people's lives who have no idea where to even begin. I work with homebuyers who are the first in their families to even be able to start the process toward homeownership. I have people who rented for a decade and are now pursuing being homebuyers.

So, I have learned that my life led me here for a reason to see that even though there are many of us doing it, my passion since day one as a little girl was to be an activist, a mentor, a counselor, and a community member who helps those in need.

OTHER DREAMS

When this Business Diva isn't working on a home loan, talking to a new homeowner, or consulting someone with questions, I am building on other projects I have. A diva should be working on other things. On herself and anything else she desires. They say to work at something that allows you to be happy, make money, and be creative. Well, starting my own boutique has made me really creative, and I find myself happy working on it. Everything we do should be because we enjoy it. Money can be made anywhere. But fulfilling the list of things I dream of and making them real is worth getting up every day.

At House of Queens, you should not only expect a boutique. My goal for the boutique is for women to feel like queens. I want to uplift all women to feel confident and empowered with the clothing that I choose or help create for

House of Queens. I will have my store online. I cannot wait to share this house with all of the queens who choose to wear my pieces. I hope to see many amazing women with different backgrounds and purposes looking beautiful in them. House of Queens will not only be a clothing boutique. A queen isn't just about her outfit, she is about her resources and tools. We need other essentials to be queens. So I will be launching a boutique with different special features that will help other queens be great.

I am at the very beginning stages and I already feel like it is a roller coaster. When I first made the jump to start my business, I went full speed, I felt unstoppable. A month later, I was beginning to get overwhelmed—I crashed mentally. There was so much going on that I was beginning to doubt myself. Should I start doing this? Why would anyone want to shop with me? I have to start smaller. I was thinking negatively. I gave myself a break; I took a week to set my mind straight. I came back to it, took it slow, and decided not to rush things. I am supposed to enjoy this, fulfill my childhood dream, and be creative.

I told myself to take my time and do what I can and see how it goes, even if it takes a long time to create and build My House of Queens. I am now planning things month to month. Most importantly, I think about my why and I know that I am young and I'm still learning and growing into the woman I will be. This is only the beginning of my story. I can't wait to see where it goes.

For women who are looking to start a business, don't be so hard on yourself and know that not everything is perfect.

Take your time and enjoy it, and always be proud of what you accomplish, no matter how big or small. Honey, slow and steady wins the race. Just as important I think is that we always remain open to change—everything in life is always changing. We must be evolving, and know it's okay because change is good. We don't want to remain in the same place forever; we want to elevate.

If it is something you really love, go for it. If it works, great, if it does not, at least you   tried it. It is not a bad thing to change your mind either. The best way to know if something is for you is by doing. But that doesn't mean you stick to it if you didn't like it. It means you keep going. As for me, I'm a young Business Diva, so my story is a glimpse of who I am becoming. Whoever she is, I know I will enjoy it, and most importantly, it will give me purpose and meaning in my life.

My Final Business Diva Word:

PERSEVERANCE

I am constantly thinking of ideas for my current business ventures, future projects I want to pursue. I am always persevering. This is how my brain works, always thinking of what the next move or project is. Once something is done, I'm thinking about what I can start working on now, who can I help next. Ever since I was a little girl, being creative and having a vision has been natural to me. I'm human, I don't always get it right the first time, but I love going after anything

I want in life. To me that is living fearless and to the fullest. To any self-starting Business Diva like me, I encourage you to keep going no matter how hard things get. We need more entrepreneurial women striving for things to make life more interesting. If I can help another Business Diva, whether it's by shopping, sharing a post, referring, or supporting in some way, count me in. I want to see more of us succeeding.

ABOUT LIZETH QUINTANA-ROMERO

Lizeth Quintana-Romero is a Mortgage Loan Expert at the #1 lending office in Illinois. She is licensed in a variety of states as well. When she is not working with a homebuyer, she is working on growing her real estate portfolio or one of her business ventures. She enjoys being a co-host for the Ambiciosas Podcast, where she discusses relevant topics. During her time, she also works along the Hispanic Regional Chamber of Commerce creating new opportunities for her community and youth.

Liz Quintana-Romero
Phone: 630-999-3760
Myhouseofqueens@gmail.com

ARIANA ROSALES

"Somos una hermosa expresión de la vida. ¡Create yourself! Créate a ti mismo."

People should stop looking at others and create their present and future. As women, we deserve the best of life, and the best comes from within ourselves. We have to look inside ourselves. We are a beautiful expression of life! We have so many qualities that we do not see; we must look inside to discover them and create them.

MY PAST: BOUNCING FROM JOB TO JOB

I was born in Lazaro Cardenas, Michoacan, Mexico. I was always a dreamer since I was a young girl. I always knew there were huge things, and I needed to discover them. My dad emphasized something very important to me growing up, "No seas conformista!"

My father's words inspired what I had in my mind, in my thoughts, and in my dreams. I knew there was something better out there for me to discover. I would see a particular style of people's lives in the city where I grew up, and I noticed there was nothing where I was from. I was in search of more!

First and foremost, I did not like school; I did not like to study. But I still wanted to grow and advance, and I looked for other strategies to accomplish what I always wanted. That is when I came to the United States. I arrived in the US when I was fifteen years of age—and I did not come alone. I had a baby in my womb, and my twenty-two-year-old sister came with me.

My first daughter, Kitzia, was born when I was sixteen. That is when the real challenge and sacrifice came. I immediately started looking for work. Since I was undocumented, I went to a traditional job and went to work at the factory. I was there temporarily; I only lasted a month. I knew this was not for me; I knew my potential and calling were bigger. I wouldn't say I liked it. I did not have documents or anything, and I had to support a baby. I worked from a traditional job; I lasted no more than two months in another factory. I was in constant movement. Then came my second child, Cesar, at eight months in 2006.

When my son came, the opportunity for a cleaning job came. I did this for extended periods; I cleaned bathrooms, blood, and casinos. I lasted one year, and finally, in 2007, I did not enjoy cleaning. I did not know how to drive then. I started driving in 2008.

I started making tamales and sold them outside of Dunkin Donuts. I would also make gorditas and other food items and sell them to tire companies. In 2008, I had my third child, my son John. I always had to bring food to the table; I had to be both mom and father. In 2009, I separated from my kids' father.

After that, it was even more complicated, and I did not ask for help from stipends or other government assistance. From 2009 to 2010, I studied as a therapist with the little money I saved. My goal was to open a spa. The little money I was saving was spent on daycare. I only had $100 left for the end of the week.

I do not know how I survived. I believe God has always been good to me. I do not know how I survived and how I continue to survive. I have seen difficult times, and I come out of them. Every time I get out, I advance. There were moments I felt I could not move, but God was always in my heart and mind, and I always asked him for strength to fall. I did fall, and would last weeks and sometimes months in depression. But I got up and went to war, because I had three people that depended on me. I have always been hard on myself.

In 2010, I had my fourth son, Raul. When I met his dad, I really wanted a son. God brought me a son. I went back to working at the factory again for about a year. Then I went to work at a supermarket. What has helped me is that I am very kind. I have been very empathetic toward people since I've experienced that empathy myself. When I speak to people, I can define and feel what people feel. In the moments when I suffered, no one was there to give me good advice. Those people, women that were supposed to teach me, always pushed me to do negative things. Bad decisions always bring negative results. In 2012, I learned about marketing and joined a company that sold roofing for home owners. It was then that I learned about the world of sales.

FROM A FAILED BUSINESS TO FINDING MY PURPOSE

My first intent in starting a business was to open a spa. It failed because I needed an understanding and tools for business. I lacked the information; my biggest fear was being undocumented. After learning marketing and sales, I sold and bought cars and was doing well. This was a world of all men, and I felt alone because I was a woman. The men saw me as an object and made me feel less than others.

I later went into a nutritional product. I was not taught marketing or business. I was in that business for two years. Then I opened a construction company on my own in 2018. Everything was going well, and that is when I saw excellent numbers. I was making great sales. However, I needed an understanding of business. I was not able to drive my business where it was needed. I had to keep growing as a business owner. One, as a business owner, has to think about the service. It is not just for one to be good and make earnings; one has to care for those supporting your business.

The sales continued to grow. I was alone and selfish, I did not want to help anyone, and wanted to take everything home. I did not want partners; I did not trust anyone. I wanted to do everything on my own. No business can be done alone; you need a team. You require people. I threw in the towel. I was exhausted!

I could not keep going. I had four kids. I was depressed from 2018 to 2019. I had thousands of dollars coming, but I was not happy. I had gained twenty pounds, was frustrated, and isolated myself from social media. I did not want to know about anyone or want anyone to know about me. Since I had gained weight, I was afraid for people to see me.

I met a person who helped. She inspired me. I realized that I enjoyed interacting with others. I worked with the same company. But I did not see any advance or any personal growth. At the same time, I began motivating myself, but I did not see any physical or emotional improvement. I just wanted to fit in. So I started a traditional job, but this job did not make me feel any better. My kids were no longer little; they now had an opinion. As soon as your kids get older, they have their own needs and wants. I began to work in an office at Dolex Dollar Express. Working at Dolex was my dream job when I came to the United States. It was a loan agency, where you worked in a nice office. But back then I did not qualify since I did not have papers or education.

My papers came in 2007! I worked for Dolex for a year. A lot of money was passing by my hands. This job reminded me I could do more, and I ended up working for someone else.

This was not for me. This was when the pandemic arrived. It was four months after the pandemic; I entered a different office job in Dec 2020. I remember I was still in depression. I was being paid $500 biweekly. I saw so much money passing my hands. I was frustrated. What was I going to do? I didn't even have to buy extra food, especially not for a month. I had nothing saved. I met my godmother, who was like an angel. She allowed me to do the business I am in now.

I did not have another option; what else was I going to do? This was the last card I could draw, so I took the opportunity. I was overwhelmed. I began to take care of myself and love myself. I had no love for myself before. I always saw others. I did not have love for myself. That is why I went to guilt, frustration, loss, pain, hurting pain, that I have done everything for others and nothing for me. That is where the phrase came from, create yourself.

I created everything, but what happened to Ariana? I began to take care of myself. I began to lose weight. I used myself as an example for a product. I was marketing my improvement. Vida Divina has changed my life. When Vida Divina came to me, I began to have a divine life.

CHANGING PEOPLE'S LIVES

With Vida Divina, I help people to change their lives from the inside. I help people who want spiritual, physical, and mental change. Through the different programs I provide, I focus on empowering women. Many women are living with depression and anxiety, as I had. I have found thousands of women in depression. What inspired me was that when I was depressed, I had no one to help me. Now that I am mentally, spiritually, and physically strong, I want to help other women. I provide nutrition to my mind, my body, and soul.

I also work on my nutrition. I began to work on myself, and I focused on myself first. You then become a magnet of attraction. You attract people who have suffered a lot and are looking for a change.

In the marketing industry, you can help and change lives and your family's lives. It improves the relationship of families, and you have a quality of life. You have peace and tranquility. If you take care of your emotional peace, you'll have balance, and if you provide nutrition to your mind, with learning. In whatever you want to grow, you begin advancing. I love reading! I realized I disliked school because I wanted to learn about life!

HUNGER AND DESIRE WERE MY PUSH

The first resource was *el hambre y las ganas*, the hunger and the desire. The second was wanting to give my children what they deserve, not what is in my hands. The third is being able to help my parents and provide them with that stability when they can no longer care for themselves. These are the strengths I use to sharpen my knife and motivation. These are my reasons; if they are good, I must keep progressing. I cannot stop.

My first mentor was God. He has always been my guide. My mentors in life have been my parents. Third, in Vida Divina, we have over twenty mentors—and they have proof of success with their own results.

I enjoy being a business owner, and I help grow other people. I help inspire other women and men, couples, single parents, and single moms and dads to stop thinking that poverty is always forever, and to start believing that there is a better world and to know oneself better. I enjoy what I do because when I see a person changing or improving, that is my biggest reward; it's not the money, nor the checks, but the smile of that person that is happy. They are leaving their bad habits behind.

My Final Word:

CREATE

Words of advice from a Business Diva: Never let anyone undermine you. First and foremost, be sure that this is the business or industry you want to be involved in. This is precisely what you want. It is not easy to have a business, but if that is what you are passionate about, and this is what moves you and makes you happy then go for it. It will always be challenging if it's something good. And if you believe in yourself, this will take you to the next level. Try not to be limited. Forget the critiques, the only person with you is yourself, and your mind will either be your best friend or your enemy.

All women are very valuable; never let anyone undermine your potential or your dignity as a woman or human. In reality, you are useful by simply being a woman, and it's just a matter of getting it out to shine.

ABOUT ARIANA ROSALES

Ariana was born in Lazaro Cardenas, Michoacan. Ariana began her entrepreneurship journey at twenty years of age. Ariana has been a professional in the networking and marketing industry since 2019. She is a mentor and leader inspiring and developing leaders for a healthy lifestyle and financial freedom.

Ariana Rosales
Phone: 312-399-2622
Ariannarogarci@gmail.com

DR. SHARON BARNES

"More than a conqueror means to me that no matter what obstacles, distractions, or challenges may come my way, I am more than equipped to overcome them."

I was born in Texas and raised in Compton, California. At thirteen years old, we moved to Pomona, California, where I went on to graduate from high school a year early. I was voted outstanding senior for that graduating year and given the honor of delivering the class baccalaureate address. Then I went straight to a four-year college and earned my degree in communications and technical business as a minor from California State Fullerton.

While in high school, I worked in the CETA program, which was an on-the-job training program enacted by President Nixon in 1973 for disadvantaged youth and adults. As a CETA participant, I provided administrative support at the Pomona Legal Aid Society, Y.M.C.A., the social services office, and the General Dynamics Aerospace company. Despite numerous applications during my youth, I was never hired by a retailer or fast-food establishment, like McDonald's or Jack in the Box. Even though they did not hire me, I was always rejected with compliments and positive character references. They always thought I was well-suited for leadership. I recall one occasion where the interviewer told me that she was not going to hire me because in six months, I would be coming after her job. I guess they always thought I was suited for more. Even as a kid, I had an "office type" personality. Except for the summer I worked at the Y.M.C.A, I was typically the only teenager in the office, and I was always working with adults.

MAKING AN IMPORTANT DECISION

I always loved school. I could barely get through the two weeks between the end of the school year and the beginning of summer school. So with extra credit from attending summer school each year, I had more than the required number of credits to graduate at the end of my junior year. I wasn't trying to graduate early, it was the school counselor who advised me that I had exceeded the requirements for graduation. I went home and told my mother what the counselor said. We discussed the core question of whether I should graduate early or continue through my senior year. The only substantive class I had left to take was physics. So, with my mother's support, I decided to graduate early.

I returned to the counselor's office to tell her that I had decided to graduate and apply to a four-year college. Her response was to strongly suggest that I apply to the local community college for two years and live at home. She questioned whether I was mature enough at seventeen years old to attend a four-year university. With a 3.8 GPA, she could not question whether I was academically prepared for the university curriculum.

I again returned to my trusted advisor, my mother, to update her on what the counselor had said and get her opinion. She has always told me that I could do whatever I put my mind to. She instilled in me the foundational principles that I have built my personal and professional life with. My mother said that the counselor did not know my character or level of maturity. My mother believed that I was more than mature enough to attend the university. That was all it took for me to proceed with my goal to go straight from high school to college.

When I went to college, I continued administrative support work with California State University, Fullerton's Upward Bound program, and the United Parcel Service (UPS). When it came time to do my college internship, I returned to my aerospace roots and applied to Hugh Aircraft Company, an aerospace company in Anaheim, California. I did my internship in technical writing and was trained by the US Army. When I graduated from college, it was only natural that my work experience in the aerospace industry was most attractive to employers in that same industry. While I was looking for a job, I interviewed with General Dynamics, the aerospace company I worked for in high school. Despite being one of the most interesting interviews of my career—

which I will further explain—General Dynamics offered me the best job proposal, so I returned to them for my first job after college.

A NEW CHAPTER

After working at General Dynamics for about a year, I decided to go back to school because I did not want to be punching a time clock until I retired. However, I could not make up my mind if I wanted to pursue a master's degree in business administration or a law degree. I applied to eight colleges for both their MBA and law programs. I was hoping the school acceptances would decide for me, but since I was admitted to each school, I was still left with the decision.

I decided to attend Southwestern School of Law in Los Angeles California because it was the best school in the area that did not have a year-long waiting list. When I decided to go to law school, I wanted to get started right away, not wait for another year. I have never been good at being idle once I have set my mind to a goal. Also, most law schools do not have a part-time program. I had to work my way through law school, so a part-time program was a necessity for considering any law school. Southwestern's part-time program required students to work a minimum of thirty hours a week and attend mandatory classes from six p.m. to nine p.m., Monday through Thursday. At the time I started law school, I was working at Northrop, another aerospace company, forty to sixty hours a week. Literally, I had the weekend to catch up on homework and all other chores of life.

THE HUSTLE CONTINUES

Some would think that I had a full plate with no time to breathe between work and school. But I guess I was having some kind of superwoman complex, because I married my husband between semesters during my first year in law school. We had a full-on wedding with more than two hundred fifty guests. Did I mention we also bought our first home in conjunction with planning our wedding?

The second year of law school became more challenging. I began to have health issues, so I transferred to Western State University School of Law in Fullerton because their part-time program was more conducive for a working adult. I graduated from Western State and passed the California State Bar Exam while still fully employed at Northop.

As mentioned earlier, when I first interviewed with General Dynamics, it was a very interesting exchange that is worth noting. The interviewer asked me various discriminatory questions, yet my expertise and determination prevailed, and not only did General Dynamics make me the best employment offer which I accepted, but the same man that asked those questions, gave me a 33 percent raise after only six months on the job. Talk about the irony! However, he would soon show me how far people would go to hinder me from achieving my goals.

Before he found out I had applied to law school, my manager showered me with praise and special projects. However, when I asked him for a letter of recommendation which I needed to complete my law application, he lost his mind. He started yelling about how lawyers were a dime a dozen, but the thing that hurt me the most was when he said, "I don't know what to say about you. So you write the letter and whatever it says, I'll sign it." This exchange was so unexpected and felt like a dart to my heart. I went to a senior coworker instead who wrote me an excellent recommendation letter.

CHOOSING ME

My first job as an attorney was with a law firm in Riverside, California, that specializes in personal injury and medical malpractice. While working at the firm, I got pregnant and was diagnosed with lupus. I had a high-risk pregnancy and I spent the majority of my pregnancy in the hospital. I was off work for ten months. But thanks be to God, the law firm kept me on the payroll and with medical insurance. I had eight surgeries in only six months. I had lost my kidneys and my daughter was born with special needs. It was a very difficult time.

When I was ready to work, the law firm allowed me to continue. I had kidney failure, which required me to go on dialysis. The law firm was very accommodating and supportive. I went back to work and did everything I could for the firm. I recall summarizing medical records and deposition transcripts during my dialysis treatment.

A few years later, the firm started having financial troubles, and I was in the second round of layoffs. With the severance pay I received, my husband and I decided to pay down some household expenses and make some extra mortgage payments. We thought this strategy would allow me time to find another job without worrying about finances.

My reality was to start a business. I had a medical condition that had no cure, and I had a child with special needs. It would have had a definite impact on the cost of medical insurance coverage for any firm. I could not convince anyone to hire me with the medical condition and a child with special needs. I had no other choice than to work on my own. I was blessed to have achieved my doctorate degree and had worked as an attorney for six years at the time. So I opened my own law office. This was my pivot into entrepreneurship. I networked with other attorneys and joined the African American Attorney Association in the Inland Empire, where I met two other attorneys. One of them said that as women, mothers, and wives, we could do better together than separately. We were the first Black female¬–owned law firm in the area. I still had my daughter at the time, and I went in business with these ladies, and it worked for a while.

TREADING FORWARD

My business partners and I all had leader personalities and different understanding of true partnership. The two other partners had a falling-out with each other, so I took over as the managing partner. However, I could not bring unity and longevity to the firm. We were never on the same page, we were not working toward a common goal, but ultimately not having the mindset of a business owner is what made us split. After we closed the firm, I once again opened another law office. My daughter passed away when she was seven in 1996. One of my former partners and friend came back to look over my practice while I adjusted after my daughter passed away.

With hard work and moving forward, I became an attorney for many major credit card companies and went from zero to thirty-five employees. Even though they were Fortune 500–level clients, I was working with small businesses and nonprofits and helping businesses get started. My heart has always been supporting my community.

I had clients that needed to get their businesses started and infrastructure activated and I helped them get their buildings too. My clients encouraged me to get a real estate license to help them with this service as well. So I went to get my real estate license as a broker, since my clients kept insisting. I started doing real estate projects not only in California, but all over the United States.

I have had the opportunity to represent California-based corporate clients in multi-state government projects regarding the commercial real estate aspect of the program operations. I have also assisted developers and investors on various real estate investment projects in numerous states. Many of my clients view my legal background to be a valued added benefit when it comes to various aspects of their real estate investments. In my office we have business development training, open to the community, and have many meetings, even prayer groups and Bible study. The Lord has brought me through difficult times and I can now be beneficial to my community.

A NEW JOURNEY

A moment of struggle I had was being a victim of identity theft from one of my key employees. At the same time, my husband had lost his sight. I had to take care of my husband and from there, I took a sabbatical from my law practice. I had to do something to take care of my family, so I decided to transition into real estate. My new career came out of many transitions and things that happened in my life. I had to fight the battle, and wherever I end up is where the Lord intended me to be.

I am currently a real estate professional with Coldwell Banker Realty, providing both residential and commercial real estate services. During the Covid-19 shutdown, I believe a lot of people started thinking differently about their living space. So I started ADU Advantage and earned my certification as an ADU Specialist from the California Association of Realtors. ADU Advantage specializes in helping homeowners who want to build accessory dwelling units (ADUs) in their backyards. The process can be overwhelming and stressful for many, so our team serves as a hub of education and resources dedicated to elevating the knowledge base regarding the process of building accessory dwelling units. Recent changes in California laws have eased a lot of the barriers to building ADUs, so more people can participate in bringing good sustainable housing for all ages. Whether you are interested in creating extra cash flow, increasing retirement funds, or housing a loved one, we guide our clients from concept to construction.

I had always taken classes and courses to continue

my development and learning. Along the way, I had many mentors too. But my main mentors were me, my husband, and my faith. My perspective about being a business owner is that it is a great tool or resource rather than having to depend on someone to give you money in exchange for time.

Being a business owner has allowed me to be successful, despite the trials and tribulations. Owning a business has allowed me to plant the seeds for others to be business owners and help make their dreams come true.

My Final Business Diva Word:

ASSET

I will tell any woman: it is an asset to have a business. Think about something you will do for free but you can monetize. The world is changing so fast that you must have a business that is based on a service or product that helps make a person's life better or helps address any situation. It has to improve someone's life and help overcome something. If not, it is not only a determinant to you and your family but to our community as a whole.

ABOUT DR. SHARON BARNES

Dr. Sharon Barnes combines more than thirty years of experience as a former attorney, entrepreneur, business owner, consultant, and real estate professional to provide knowledge and resources to propel her clients to the next level. At ADU Advantage, we educate, train, support, and help you develop real estate you already own and control. Drawing from years of experience, the company has the expertise to elevate the knowledge base of the community regarding the process of building an access dwelling unit (ADU), so more people can participate in bringing good sustainable housing for all ages.

As a Certified ADU Specialist, Dr. Sharon Barnes is uniquely positioned to help homeowners and developers understand site eligibility, local regulations, development process and costs, and the return on investment of ADUs. ADU Advantage and its team are highly sought after by clients who seek to build access dwelling units (ADUs) as a vital affordable and sustainable housing solution for low- to moderate-income communities. Many of their clients choose to utilize ADUs as a means to start building generational wealth through real estate investment.

Their services include education and training, residential and commercial real estate, investing, development, and many other resources. ADU Advantage is an environmentally responsible and resource-efficient conscious as evidenced by the Green Designation earned by Dr. Sharon Barnes from the National Association of Realtors.

Their green sustainable building practice expands throughout a building's life cycle: from design, construction, operation, maintenance, and renovation. Making sure our clients understand their options and have the needed knowledge to make informed decisions throughout the process is the cornerstone of their real estate development and consultant practice.

Dr. Sharon Barnes
Founder, CEO, Certified ADU Specialist, Real Estate Professional and GREEN Designee
www.aduadvantagenow.com
FB: @ADUAdvantageCA & @DrSharonBarnesRealEstate
aduadvantgeca@gmail.com

ANA RODRIGUEZ

"Legacy is not what's left tomorrow when you're gone. It's what you give, create, impact, and contribute today while you are here that then happens to live on"
—Rasheed Ogunlaru

If you had told me fifteen years ago that I would be making delicious cakes for a living, I would be saying no way! As a child, I never had a specific career dream. As a teenager, I believed I could contribute to my community by becoming a social worker. College was my goal after high school. I even obtained a grant, but unfortunately, due to circumstances out of my control, it didn't go as planned.

At the time, I was working at an office downtown. I had a 9-to-5, and I thought that would be my future. It must have been destiny because one day, leaving my office job, I saw a Help Wanted job sign in a downtown café/bakery. I walked in and inquired about it. I thought it would be a good opportunity for additional income, but little did I know that it would spark interest in the baking industry.

I once had a bad experience at a local bakery ordering my nephew's birthday cake. As I was picking up my order, I noticed they made a mistake by giving me a bigger cake than what I had originally ordered, and they also charged me for their mistake. I was upset and asked them to review my order because that was not what I had ordered. To my surprise, the employee disagreed with me and said there was nothing she could do for me, as she was being rude and unprofessional. I wanted them to correct their mistake and acknowledge me as a client. But it was a horrible experience, and I had to pay for the bigger cake. I made a promise to myself and decided I was going to learn how to bake and prepare the cakes myself. Working as a supervisor at the café also made me more interested in learning the ins and outs of running a business. I felt like I was fitting in, and I loved the feeling of being surrounded by people and delicious baked goods. I quit my office job and committed full-time to the café.

While working at the café, I enrolled in a Master Cake decorating class. I was serious about learning about the process and insights to help my baking career journey. At that time, I had two goals in mind: raising my kids and starting my small business from home, which would give me the perfect opportunity to be able to be with my kids as much as possible but also grow in my profession.

After two years at the café, I was unfortunately fired. As I started practicing at home and baking more on my own, the owner found out I was building my own customer base in the baking business. I was discovering my baking passion. It was a conflict of interest according to her. It was very hurtful and disappointing, but I understood her decision. I loved that job; it taught me how to run a business. I had a work family I loved and a sense of belonging, but I think it was for the best. However, at that moment I was more determined to move forward and find out where this journey might take me. My energy was now all focused on baking and gaining experience on my own. I consider myself a self-taught baker.

My husband has been my biggest support in this journey, and although at the beginning it was not easy, I knew in my heart it was not impossible. I felt confident and, at the same time, very uneasy about starting a home baking business. My children were small and needed my attention 100 percent. I struggled to balance work, family time, and sometimes emergency visits when my kids were sick, and I didn't want to lose myself in the process. Some days were better than others, but I always told myself I was doing it for my family. We have to eliminate the guilt and embrace the struggle to survive the days when we feel we are not doing enough. You can be a good mother and still follow your dreams.

I started learning by reading books on techniques and a variety of recipes. The recipes from the books were my number-one resource. I started promoting my business by showing up at friends' parties with a cake or pastries. Then I made business cards and created social media pages to show my work, which was a huge stepping-stone in this journey to a more sustainable business. I started creating my list of flavors, sharing photos of my work on social media, and promoting my work with friends.

I would be asked by friends of friends to make small cakes for them, mostly for birthdays. Once they tasted a few different cakes, they would come back to order more, and bigger cakes for different occasions. Spring was my busy season for religious cakes and graduation cakes, and summer was my wedding season. But all year round, there were birthdays to celebrate and important milestones captured with a custom cake and shared on social media.

Anniversaries and baby showers would follow after the wedding cakes. Those orders from the same clients would make me very happy, knowing that they would continue to order year after year on those special dates for them. Many times, I wanted to give up, and many times I felt extremely exhausted, and things didn't always go as planned. Sometimes I would be late on my orders, get sick with stress, and barely make any profit.

I knew my work was good, but at times I lacked the confidence to charge more for fear of rejection. Consistency and hard work make the difference, NEVER GIVE UP. We as women never give ourselves enough credit and forget it's OK not to be perfect. We must make mistakes to get better, to grow personally and professionally. I have had my share of mistakes. I have made so many errors with my orders. I have screwed up dates for cake orders, the inscriptions, and the flavors, and I have owned my mistakes. I have felt terrible, I have been yelled at many times by people who think there is no room for error, and instead of letting that break me, it has made me stronger and more valiant. I have learned to change my mindset, to trust I am doing my best, to forget the mistake and remember the lesson.

Working in the baking industry is extremely overwhelming. Trying to perfect your techniques, keeping up with the trends, and making clients happy one cake at a time is challenging. Consistency is key. Like any other job, running your own business is hard, but not impossible. We don't see it, but as time passes by, we make progress and undeniably get better. We must keep motivating ourselves and not give up. My clients come back year after year for all their special celebration cakes, and that makes me feel confident that I'm doing something right. I give 110 percent to my business.

My family has been my rock in all of this. Without them, I'm nothing! My family has believed in me since day one. I'm especially thankful and grateful for my dad, who has worked tirelessly to give us a better life, at times working two jobs and keeping us safe and comfortable from any troubles. My dad is involved in my business as my delivery man. I cannot express the gratitude and admiration I have for my parents. They cheer on my accomplishments and stand by my side when I need them.

I have a vivid image in my head of when I was in the fourth grade. My dad would sit with me after a long day at work to help me with my homework. Math was the hardest, and I would cry because I wouldn't get it. My dad would explain patiently over and over again until I would finally get it right, several nights in a row for the entire school year. I'm so grateful he didn't give up on me or punish me for taking his time. I think those moments of desperation between a child and a parent are hard, but inevitably shape you as you get older.

Now, as a parent and business owner, I'm grateful and humbled by those moments. I'm patient with my kids and, in my profession, tolerant and understanding when stressful situations occur. They motivate and help me to accomplish my goals. It sure takes a village to be a boss. Your team becomes the bones of the business! They are the ones that take the burn and long hours working their magic to make the end project a success. I have connected and reconnected with so many amazing people. Many have helped me expand my clientele, some my knowledge in the business industry, and others have shown me the importance of community empowerment. I would like to spread the word about programs and organizations that have been extremely important in the growth of my business, the people who push for grants for minority-owned businesses like mine.

In 2018, I took my first course at Mujeres Latinas in Acción called "Curso de Empresarios del Futuro" alongside ten other small business entrepreneurs. That program was such an amazing experience because it helped me formalize my small home business. After completing that program, they referred me to the amazing Little Village Chamber of Commerce, where I took part in their "Juntos Emprendemos" program for small businesses. The program helped with proper registration of my business and technical assistance in the areas of legal, accounting, and finance. I received a grant for equipment for my business, and also a grant for creating a website, including mentorship in marketing and social media.

I'm truly grateful for all the help I have received to better my business, and I think we can give the same advice to someone who is starting a new business. Communities working together empower our future generations and establish roots and a foundation for future entrepreneurs.

Congratulate yourself on constantly showing up, even when things seem to be failing; a little progress each day adds up to big results. My biggest piece of advice is to not be afraid to ask for help. As silly as it might be, ask the question, because there are so many professionals with experience and knowledge willing to help. I am proud to have created a business from zero, creating an identity for my business and sharing my delicious cakes and pastries with the world.

My parents shaped me into the woman I am today. Their guidance, love, and discipline are the best recipe to forge my own path and live a life of fulfillment and making the necessary mistakes and choices to get there. For me, it is important to leave a legacy behind. I'm not referring to assets or money. For me, it's more about memories and learning experiences. My children have gained so much knowledge about the baking world and the work involved in running a business. The more people that get to know me, the more that will remember me by my work, and the anecdotes about all the cakes ordered for their most special celebrated moments.

Cakes are the symbol of sweetness and celebration. There's magic and wishes and happy emotions! But most importantly, love. And I cannot imagine life without delicious cakes.

I have built the most loyal customer base because they keep ordering from me. I keep expanding and growing as a business with much success. I'm happy with what I have constructed and learned so far. I continue perfecting my craft and never stop practicing. Every cake I bake and decorate takes a tiny piece of my time and my passion for the craft because good things take time.

My Final Business Diva Word:

PASSION

My Business Diva Word is passion. I bake and forget about it all. I forget how tired my body is, I forget to eat, to take a break, to mentally separate myself from work. I have truly found my passion, what drives me. I reflect my love for baking. I ask you: what is your passion? The things you are passionate about are not random; they are your calling.

ABOUT ANA RODRIGUEZ

Ana E. Rodriguez was born in Celaya Guanajuato, Mexico. She is the oldest of four siblings.

She came to Chicago at the age of nine and lived in the Pilsen neighborhood with her family. She is a certified cake decorator from the Wilton School of Cake Decorating and Confectionary Art. Ana is a successful entrepreneur and owner of Sophie's Cakes and Pastries. Her highlights for this year include baking birthday cakes for two celebrities, one of them being the worldwide-known artist Bad Bunny.

Ana is very involved in her community, making time to be a motivational speaker at schools for career day. Prior to the pandemic, she was a member of the nonprofit organization Golden Smiles, led by a group of business owners organizing celebration parties at senior homes, providing breakfast, lunch, pastries, music, and a fun show to bring them happiness and joy.

Her purpose is to keep connecting with other entrepreneurs, change the economic structure in the community, create jobs, and support and empower women. She is married with three children, Victor, Sophia, and Alexandra, who are her everyday inspiration.

Ana Rodriguez
anita_baker25@yahoo.com
www.sophiescakesandpastries.com
IG: @sophiescakesandpastries

ABOUT THE AUTHOR

Martha Razo

MATHEMATICIAN

Martha Razo graduated from Illinois Institute of Technology with a Bachelors and Masters in Applied Mathematics with a focus in Statistics.

AUTHOR

Martha has been featured in the following books:

- *Today's Inspired Latina Volume X*
- *Business Diva*
- *Latinas in Finance launching in January of 2023.*
- *Today's Inspired Leader Volume IV launching January of 2023.*
- *Latinx Community Awards Leaders launching December 2022.*
- *Fire Up Connect Book*

And featured in various magazines:
- *Fire-Up Connect* Magazine – Front cover feature, "How I used the Power of Numbers to grow a multi-million dollar company and how I help business owners due the same."
- *Top 100 Business Entrepreneurs*
- *My Dream* Act Play launching in 2023.

ENGINEER

Martha is a researcher with numerous publications in academic papers in artificial intelligence and process mining which you can find all in Google Scholar.

FINANCIAL COACH

Martha is a finance coach, through World Financial Group to help families build generation wealth.

BUSINESS OWNER

Martha is the founder and CEO of SOLiX, which consults business owners and helps them grow their business using a data-based approach to build business strategy.

TEACHER

Martha is a teacher, and she teaches The Power of Numbers Course offered twice a year. It's a 6-week course that shows business owners the key business numbers, financial reports, forecasts and breakeven price to grow their businesses.

PHILANTHROPIST

Martha is a philanthropist, she co- founded the 2% Fund, which awards scholarships to undocumented students all over the US and provides mentorship.

OWNER OF DREAM NUTRITION CAFE

Martha is co-owner of Dream Nutrition Café located in the Edgewater neighborhood of Chicago. If you are in the Chicagoland area, be sure to visit Martha and come. It is an amazing space for conducting business, having meetings, and having a nice healthy breakfast or brunch.

RADIO HOST FOR FABULOUS LIFESTYLE RADIO SHOW

Martha is a Radio Host for KCAA radio broadcasted on 106.5 FM and 1050 am. Martha talks about FINANCE every 3rd Sunday of the month at 2pm PST or 5pm CST. The show is recorded and streamed on iHeart Radio, Roku, Apple play and has a reach of over 5 million people. Martha had the pleasure of speaking to many business owners all over the world.

CO-HOST ENTRE NOSOTRAS

Martha is the co-host of Entre Nosotras with Edna Rodriguez, the brain behind Entre Nosotras, and Imelda Rodriguez. She has had the privilege of interviewing many Hollywood artists such as Alejandro de Hoyos, who is the principal actor and producer of the movie, "El Contratista", Alejandro Marin, who was the brain behind the film, *The Wrong Guy,* and also Doreen Calderon, actress of Please Hold, which was nominated for an Academy award. Others include, Carla Roda, award-winning director. Furthermore, they bring value to the Spanish speaking community by bringing community leaders to discuss topics such as cyber security, relationship building, health and nutrition awareness, business and financial resources and more.

INVESTOR

Martha is an investor and co-owner of Gitana Properties and Razo Properties.

Martha the MOM

Martha is a mother to Angelo Vazquez; he is a ray of sunshine in her life. From Martha, "He does not know this but being his mother has taught me so many, patience, which I did not seem to have learned from my mom."

Connect with Martha!
SOLiX Business Services
solixbizservices@gmail.com
Phone: 312-523-5561
www.martharazo.com

Guero's Pallets, Inc.
gueropallets1@gmail.com

Made in the USA
Monee, IL
08 December 2022

20329393R00131